The Know-It-All

A Resource for Kids and Grown-ups

Patricia R. Peterson

Illustrations by Stephen Schudlich

Good Year Books

An Imprint of Addison-Wesley Educational Publishers, Inc.

Dedication

To Phil

Good Year Books

are available for most basic curriculum subjects plus many enrichment areas. For more Good Year Books, contact your local bookseller or educational dealer. For a complete catalog with information about other Good Year Books, please write:

Good Year Books
1900 East Lake Avenue
Glenview, IL 60025

Design by Anello Design, Chicago.
Copyright © 1998 Good Year Books.
All Rights Reserved.
Printed in the United States of America.

ISBN 0-673-36377-5
  2 3 4 5 6 7 8 9 - CRK - 04 03 02 01 00 99 98

Preface

Do you need help but your teacher is busy? Has it been so long since you've learned a skill that you've forgotten exactly what to do? Are you "stuck" doing your homework, and you don't know what comes next? *The Know-It-All* can help.

The Know-It-All contains definitions, facts, and examples of "how to do it" about most topics studied at school. It has a wealth of interesting information about a variety of topics related to school subjects that will help extend your learning. Because the book is written in easy-to-understand language, you will have no trouble teaching yourself.

The Know-It-All is easy to use:

•Every entry is listed alphabetically.

•Every entry includes the meaning of the term.

  Most entries include examples and/or illustrations.

• *The Know-It-All* works like a dictionary.

That's all there is to it!

The Know-It-All will become one of your best friends. In fact, it will seem to grow as you grow. When you are ready to learn new things, *The Know-It-All* will be ready to teach you. If you learn one new thing every day, in one year you'll learn 365 new things; in two years, 730 new things; and in three years, 1,095 new things. Think about it!

Have fun learning and using *The Know-It-All!*

Patricia R. Peterson

P.S. It's for grown-ups, too!

Contents

A

A/An/And................................ 1
Abbreviation 2
Accent Mark 3
Accept/Except...................... 3
Acute Angle......................... 3
A.D. 3
Addend................................. 4
Addition 4
Addressing an Envelope...... 5
Adjacent Angles.................. 5
Adjective 5
Adverb................................. 6
Affect/Effect........................ 7
Algorithm 7
Alliteration 7
All Ready/Already 7
All Together/Altogether 7
Almanac 8
Alphabet.............................. 8
Alphabetizing 9
A.M. (ante meridiem) 9
Among/Between 10
Analogy 10
Angle 10
Animal Offspring 12
Annuity 12
Anonymous......................... 12
Antecedent 12
Antonym 13
Apex 13

Apostrophe........................... 13
Appendix 16
Appositive 16
Arc 16
Area 17
Array 17
Art Elements 18
Article 18
Associative Property 18
Asymmetric 18
Atlas................................... 19
Atmospheric Layers 19
Attribute 19
Autobiography..................... 19
Average 20
Axis.................................... 20

B

Ballad 21
Bank Check 21
Bar Graph 22
Base Word 22
B.C. 22
B.C.E. 23
Bedrock.............................. 23
Bibliography 23
Bill of Rights...................... 24
Biography 24
Blend 25
Book Parts 25
Book Report........................ 26

Borrowing........................... 27
B.P. 28
Brackets.............................. 28
Business Letter 28

C

Cabinet............................... 28
Calculator 29
Calendar 29
Can/May............................. 31
Capacity 31
Capital 31
Capital Letter 31
Cardinal Number 35
Carrying.............................. 36
Casting Out Nines............... 37
Celsius Thermometer 39
Centimeter 39
Chord 40
Cinquain 40
Circle.................................. 40
Circumference 40
Clause 41
Clef.................................... 42
Cliché 42
Closed Figure..................... 43
Clouds................................ 43
Clustering........................... 44
Colon 44
Colonies.............................. 44
Comma 44

Common Factor **47**
Commutative Property **47**
Compass Rose **47**
Complementary Angle **48**
Compound Interest **48**
Compound Sentence **48**
Compound Subject **48**
Compound Word **49**
Computer Words **49**
Concave **51**
Concentric Circles **51**
Congruent Figures **52**
Conjunction **52**
Consonant **52**
Consonant Cluster **53**
Constellation **53**
Continent **53**
   Map of Continents **54**
Contraction **55**
Convex **55**
Coordinates **55**
Core **55**
Counterclockwise **55**
Court System **56**
Crust **56**

D

Days of the Week **56**
Decimal **56**
Declarative Sentence **59**
Degree **59**

Denominator **60**
Desert/Dessert **60**
Dewey Decimal System **60**
Diagram **60**
Diameter **61**
Diamonte **61**
Dictionary **62**
Difference **62**
Digestive System **62**
Digit **63**
Digraph **63**
Diphthong **64**
Distributive Property **64**
District of Columbia **64**
Dividend **64**
Divisibility **64**
Division **66**
Divisor **67**

E

Earth's Layers **67**
Earthquake **68**
Ecology **68**
Edit **68**
Ellipsis **68**
Encyclopedia **68**
English/Metric
   Conversion Table **68**
Epicenter **69**
Epilogue **69**
Equator **69**

Equilateral Triangle **69**
Equinox **69**
Equivalent **69**
Essay **70**
Estimate **70**
Even Number **70**
Exclamation Point **70**
Exclamatory Sentence **70**
Expanded Numeral **70**
Exponent **70**

F

Fact Family **71**
Fact or Opinion **71**
Factor **71**
Factor Tree **71**
Fahrenheit Thermometer **72**
Farther/Further **72**
Fault **72**
Fiction **72**
Flow Chart **73**
Food Pyramid **73**
Footnote **73**
Foreign Words and
   Phrases **74**
Fossil **75**
Fraction **75**
Fraction Number Line **76**
Fraction to Decimal **76**
Free Verse **77**
Friendly Letter **77**

G

Galaxy **77**

Geographic Terms **78**

Geography **80**

Geometric Figures **80**

Glacier **82**

Glossary **82**

Good/Well **82**

Googol **82**

Graph **82**

Great Lakes **83**

Greater Than **83**

Greatest Common

   Factor (GCF) **83**

Greek Gods and

   Goddesses **84**

Greenwich Mean Time **85**

Grid **85**

Gross **85**

Guide Words **86**

H

Haiku **87**

Hemisphere **88**

Homograph **88**

Homonym **88**

Homophone **88**

Horizontal Line **88**

Hydrosphere **89**

Hyperbole **89**

Hyphen **89**

Hypotenuse **90**

I

I/Me **90**

Ibid. **90**

Idiom **91**

Igneous Rock **91**

Imperative Sentence **91**

Improper Fraction **91**

Index **92**

Inference **92**

Infinity **92**

Initial **92**

Integer **93**

Interest **93**

Interjection **93**

International Date Line **94**

Internet Words **94**

Interrogative Sentence **95**

Intersecting Lines **96**

Irregular Verb **96**

Isosceles Triangle **96**

Italics **96**

Its/It's **96**

K

Key (map) **97**

Key Signature **97**

Key Words **97**

L

Latitude **98**

Lattice Multiplication **98**

Lava **98**

Lay/Lie **99**

Leap Year **99**

Learn/Teach **99**

Least Common Denominator

   (LCD) **99**

Legend (map) **100**

Less Than **100**

Let/Leave **100**

Letter Writing (business) **101**

Letter Writing (friendly) **102**

Library of Congress

   Classification System **103**

Light Year **104**

Limerick **104**

Line Segment **104**

Longitude **105**

M

Magic Square **105**

Magma **105**

Main Topic and Subtopics .. **105**

Mantle **106**

Map **106**

Map Scale of Miles **107**

Mass **107**

Math Symbols **108**

May/Can **108**

Mean **108**

Measurement **109**

Median **109**

Meridian **110**

Metamorphic Rock **110**

Metaphor **110**

Metric/English Conversion
Table **111**

Milky Way **111**

Mineral **111**

Minuend **111**

Mixed Number **111**

Modifier **111**

Money **112**

Months of the Year **112**

Multiple **112**

Multiplicand **113**

Multiplication **113**

Multiplication Table **114**

Multiplier **116**

Musical Expressions **116**

Musical Note and Rest
Values **116**

N

N-gon **117**

Nanosecond **117**

Negative Number **117**

Net Profit **117**

Nonfiction **117**

Northwest Territory **117**

Note/Piano Key
Relationship **118**

Noun **118**

Number Line **119**

Number Pair **119**

Number Prefixes **119**

Number Sentence **119**

Numeral **119**

Numerator **120**

O

Oblong **120**

Obtuse Angle **120**

Ocean **121**

Octagon **121**

Octave **121**

Odd Number **121**

Onomatopoeia **121**

Opinion **121**

Ordered Pair **121**

Ordinal Number **122**

Outline **122**

Oxidation **123**

Oxymoron **123**

Ozone Layer **123**

P

Palindrome **123**

Pangaea **123**

Parable **124**

Paragraph **124**

Parallel Lines **125**

Parentheses **125**

Parenthetical Expression **125**

Parts of Speech **126**

Past Tense **126**

Pentagon **126**

Percent **126**

Perimeter **128**

Period **128**

Periodic Table of Elements ..**129**

Perpendicular Lines **130**

Personification **130**

Photosynthesis **130**

Phrase **130**

Pi **130**

Pitch **131**

Place Value **131**

Planet **131**

Plates **133**

Plot **133**

Plural **133**

P.M. (*post meridiem*) **135**

Possessive Nouns **135**

Predicate **135**

Prefix **136**

Preposition **137**

Prepositional Phrase **137**

Present Tense **137**

Presidential Succession
Order **138**

Presidents of the
  United States **139**
Primary Colors **140**
Prime Meridian..................**140**
Prime Number **140**
Probability **141**
Product **141**
Prologue..................**141**
Pronoun **142**
Pronunciation Key **142**
Proofreading Symbols **143**
Properties of Numbers **144**
Prose **144**
Protractor..................**144**
Proverb **145**

Q

Quadrant **145**
Quadrilateral **145**
Quatrain **145**
Quotation **146**
Quotation Marks..................**146**
Quotient **147**

R

Radius..................**148**
Ratio..................**148**
Rational Number **148**
Ray..................**148**
Reciprocal..................**148**

Rectangle **148**
Remainder..................**149**
Research Paper **149**
Rhombus **149**
Richter Scale **150**
Right Angle..................**150**
Roman Numerals **150**
Root Word..................**151**
Rounding..................**151**
Run-on Sentence **152**

S

Satire..................**152**
Scale **152**
Scalene Triangle **152**
Schwa **152**
Seasons of the Year **153**
Sector..................**153**
Sedimentary Rock **154**
Semicolon..................**154**
Sentence **154**
Sequence..................**155**
Silent Letter **155**
Simile..................**156**
Simple Interest..................**156**
Singular **156**
Solar System **156**
Solstice **156**
Sonnet **158**
Spelling Rules **158**
Spoonerism **162**

Square Root..................**162**
Staff..................**162**
States..................**162**
Stock Market..................**162**
Story Elements..................**163**
Straight Angle **163**
Stress Mark **163**
Subject..................**164**
Subject/Verb Agreement.....**164**
Subtopic **164**
Subtraction..................**164**
Subtrahend **165**
Suffix..................**166**
Sum..................**166**
Summary **167**
Supplementary Angle **167**
Syllable **167**
Symmetry **169**
Synonym **169**
Synopsis **169**
Syntax..................**169**

T

Table of Contents 170
Tangram 170
Teach 170
Tectonic Plates 170
Term Paper 170
Tessellation 171
Than/Then 171
Their/There/They're............171
Thermometer 172
Thesaurus..........................172
Tides 172
Time..................................172
Time Line 174
Time Signature 174
Time Zones 174
To/Too/Two 175
Topic Sentence....................175
Tropic of Cancer 175
Tropic of Capricorn 175

U

Underlining 176
Unit 176
United States
    Court System 176
United States of America 177
    List of the States............178

V

Venn Diagram......................180
Verb 180
Verb, Irregular 182
Vertex 183
Vertical Line......................183
Volcano 184
Volume..............................184
Vowel 184
Vowel Digraph 184

W

Weather/Whether 185
Webbing 185
Well 185
We're/Where/Were 185
Who/Whom 186
Whole Number....................186
World................................186
Writer's Word List..............187
Writing Process 188

Z

Zip Code............................189
Zodiac................................189

Activity Pages 191

Index 210

a/an/and

The words *a* and *an* are used as adjectives before other adjectives, adverbs, and singular nouns. A singular noun means one: one person, one place, one thing. The word *and* is used to connect words, phrases, or clauses.

▶ Use *a* before words beginning with a consonant and with words having a long *u* sound.

Examples: *a* funny clown
a banana
a useful tool
a unicorn

▶ Use *an* before words beginning with vowels and words beginning with a silent *h*.

Examples: *an* elephant
an old lady
an hour
an honorable person

▶ Use *and* to connect nouns, verbs, adjectives, adverbs, phrases, or clauses.

Examples: salt *and* pepper
in the house *and* in the yard
Paul played, *and* Jim studied.

abbreviation | A shortened form of a word or phrase. Abbreviations are usually followed by a period. Some abbreviations must be capitalized.

▶ Two-letter abbreviations for names of states in the United States are not followed by a period.

Examples: IL Illinois   NY New York

▶ Abbreviations of governmental agencies, labor unions, and other such organizations are not followed by a period.

Examples: FBI   NASA   AMA

▶ Abbreviations are not used in business letters or other formal correspondence.

Common Abbreviations

A.D. ...... *anno Domini*	**etc.** .... *et cetera;* and so forth	**Mrs.** .... Mistress
adj. .... adjective		**Ms.** ...... Miss or Mrs.
adv. .... adverb	**fig.** .... figure	**n.** .... noun
A.M. ... *ante meridiem;* before noon	**ft** .... foot	**oz** .... ounce
	gal. .... gallon	**P.M.** .... *post meridiem;* after noon
anon. ...... anonymous	**Gov.** .... Governor	
ant. .... antonym	**hr** .... hour	**P.O.** .... post office
Ave. .... Avenue	**ht.** .... height	**P.S.** .... postscript
B.C. ...... before Christ	**hwy.** .... highway	**pt** .... pint
biog. ...... biography	**i.e.** ...... *id est;* that is	**qt** .... quart
Blvd. .... Boulevard	**illus.** ...... illustration	**Rd.** .... Road
Capt. .... Captain	**in.** .... inch	**Rev.** .... Reverend
C.E.O. .... Chief Executive Officer	**inc.** ...... incorporated	**R.S.V.P.** .... *Répondez, s'il vous plaît;* please respond
	Jr. .... Junior	
cm .... centimeter	**k** .... kilo	
C.O.D. .... collect on delivery	**kg** .... kilogram	**St.** .... Street
	l .... liter	**syn.** .... synonym
conj. ...... conjunction	**lb** .... pound	**USA** ..... United States of America
cont. .... continued	**liq.** .... liquid	
corp. ...... corporation	**M.D.** .... *medicinae doctor*	**v.** .... verb
D.C. .... District of Columbia		**VIP** .... Very Important Person
	mi .... mile	
dept. ...... department	**misc.** ... miscellaneous	**vol.** .... volume
Dr. .... Doctor	**mph** .... miles per hour	**vs.** .... versus
doz. .... dozen	**Mr.** .... Mister	**yd** .... yard

See also **United States of America.**

accent mark	A mark used in a pronunciation guide to show which syllable of a word is said or heard loudest. That syllable is called the primary accented syllable.

Examples: pen´ - cil   *2 syllables*
a - bove´   *2 syllables*
re - mem´- ber   *3 syllables*

 Help!

▶ Underlining accented syllables will help you pronounce the word more easily.

accept/except	The word *accept* is a verb that means "to take as true" or "to agree to."

Example: I will *accept* your answer.

The word *except* means "to leave out," "other than," or "but."

Examples: I passed every test *except* one.
Everyone can meet at noon *except* Joe.

acute angle	*See* **angle.**

A.D.	An abbreviation for the Latin words *anno Domini* (in the year of the Lord), meaning the time in years *after* the birth of Christ.

Help!

▶ A.D. 1997 means one thousand nine hundred ninety-seven years after the birth of Christ.

▶ A.D. is often omitted in modern times. A date written without the letters is assumed to be A.D.

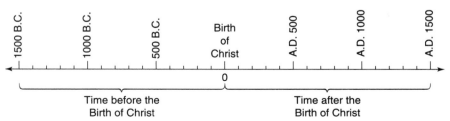

See also **B.C.**

addend   A number to be added; any of a set of numbers to be added.

Examples: 7
            +2

The numbers 7 and 2 are **addends.**

            3
            9
            +12

The numbers 3, 9, and 12 are **addends.**

addition   The process of adding a number to one or more numbers. The answer is called the **sum.**

Example: 5
            2   or 5 + 2 + 3 = 10
            +3
            10   The number ten is the **sum.**

▶ Words used to signal addition problems.

add	increase	how many all together
sum	plus	how much was added
total	addend	put together

Try these shortcuts to add faster.

▶ Find groups of ten in column addition.

Example: 58
            164 ⎞ = 10
            322 ⎠ = 10
            + 56

▶ Add the value of the tens column first. Then add the value of the units column to the total.

Example: To add 36 + 47, think:

3 tens + 4 tens = 7 tens   or   **70**
6 ones + 7 ones = 13 ones or **+13**
                              83

See also **casting out nines.**

addressing an envelope

See **letter writing.**

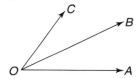

adjacent angles   Either of two angles that share a common side and a common vertex (point).

∠ AOB and ∠ BOC are adjacent angles and share $\overrightarrow{OB}$ (ray) as their common side.

adjective   A word that describes or tells about a person, place, or thing. Adjectives tell what kind, which one, or how many.

Examples:

What Kind	Which One	How Many
tiny toes	*that* box	*several* men
large city	*this* house	*few* pigs
bright sun	*those* girls	*both* ladies
lazy boy	*these* pencils	*all* children

Three Degrees of Comparative Adjectives

1. Regular

   An adjective that shows no comparison, describes one thing.

   a *soft* pillow

2. Comparative

An adjective that shows comparison between two things.

the *softer* pillow

3. Superlative

An adjective that shows the greatest comparison among three or more things.

the *softest* pillow

▶ Colors and numbers are usually adjectives.

▶ For adjectives of three or more syllables, use *more* or *most*.

Example:

more disappointed   *most* disappointed

Irregular Forms of Comparative and Superlative Adjectives

Regular	Comparative	Superlative
bad	worse	worst
far	farther	farthest
good	better	best
little	less	least
many	more	most
much	more	most

adverb

A word that tells how, when, where, how much, or how often something happens. Adverbs often end in *-ly*. Adverbs describe verbs, adjectives, other adverbs, and sentences. They are often found at the end of a sentence.

Examples: Karen finished her work *quickly*.
He *finally* went home.
Where is my ruler?
Mom was *very* late.
They called home quite *frequently*.
Fortunately, Sam found the key.

▶ Adverbs that tell "to what extent" are called **intensifiers**.

Intensifiers

almost	quite
extremely	rather
less	so
more	somewhat
most	too

affect/effect

The word *affect* is usually used as a verb meaning "to have an influence on."

Example: Cold, rainy weather *affects* my mood.

The word *effect* is a noun meaning "the result."

Example: The effect of eating good food is to produce a healthy body.

algorithm

A step-by-step set of instructions for solving a problem.
See example in **division** *for* **long division.**

alliteration

The repetition of the beginning sound in each word.

Examples: Miss Molly mashed her meat with a mighty mallet.
Eric eats early every evening.

all ready/already

The words *all ready* mean that everything is prepared; set to use.

Example: We're *all ready* for the parade to begin.

The word *already* is an adverb. It means "before this time."

Example: I've seen that movie *already.*

all together/ altogether

The words *all together* mean "gathered or collected together."

Example: When we worked *all together,* we collected $100 for charity.

The word *altogether* is an adverb meaning "completely."

Example: The class was *altogether* too noisy.

almanac   A book published yearly that lists a collection of facts, tables, graphs, and information on many subjects and events, arranged in alphabetical order. Use an almanac for information about these topics:

accidents and disasters	populations
awards	sports records
history and government	weather
music and art	world news

alphabet   The letters of a written language arranged in order.

Examples:

Manuscript Writing

Aa Bb Cc Dd Ee Ff Gg Hh Ii Jj Kk Ll Mm Nn
Oo Pp Qq Rr Ss Tt Uu Vv Ww Xx Yy Zz

Cursive Writing

Aa Bb Cc Dd Ee Ff Gg Hh Ii Jj Kk Ll Mm Nn
Oo Pp Qq Rr Ss Tt Uu Vv Ww Xx Yy Zz

alphabetizing | Putting letters or words in alphabetical (A-B-C) order.

▶ List by *first* letters all words to be alphabetized.

Examples: apple
banana
coconut

▶ If all the first letters are the same, alphabetize by the *second* letter.

Examples: peach
plum
pumpkin

▶ If the first letter *and* the second letter are the same, alphabetize by the *third* letter.

Examples: pickle
pineapple
pizza

▶ Use this same method if the first three letters are the same, and continue until the letters do not match.

▶ When alphabetizing people's first and last names, list the *last* name first, followed by a comma, and then write the first name and initial. Then also alphabetize by order of first name.

Examples: Jones, Phillip R.
Jones, Raymond P.
Jones, W. C.

A.M.
(ante meridiem) | Used to show time from after midnight to noon.

Examples: 2:10 A.M.   8:30 A.M.   11:59 A.M.

among/between | The word *among* is used when someone is speaking of three or more things.

> **Example:** Haley divided her stickers *among* the four of us.

The word *between* is used when speaking of just two things.

> **Example:** Haley divided her stickers between Eric and Sandy.

analogy | A comparison between two different words or things that shows how they are alike.

> **Examples:** Hot is to cold as summer is to winter. (Opposites)
>
> Needle is to sew as pen is to write. (What the objects are used for)
>
> Finger is to hand as toe is to foot. (Part of a larger thing)

Recognize an analogy by the use of the words "is to" or "is like" and "as".

The symbol : is sometimes used for the words "is to."
The symbol :: is sometimes used for the word "as."

> **Example:** baby : babies :: cooky : cookies   (Singular/Plural)

angle [∠] | The space formed when two straight lines touch at the same point.

The point is called the vertex, and the lines are called rays. The symbol for a ray is $\overrightarrow{AB}$. The symbol for an angle is ∠.

B
C —————— *D*

When letters are used to name an angle, the vertex (point) is placed between the line (ray) letters. The following is angle ∠*BCD:*

Help!

1. Angles are measured in degrees (°) with a protractor.

2. When measuring an angle, remember to measure the space between the lines and not the length of the lines.

3. Line up the center of a protractor (90°) with the vertex of the angle and one side of the angle. Be sure one side of the angle is on the 0° mark.

4. To find the measurement of the angle, read the degrees where the other line of the angle crosses the protractor.

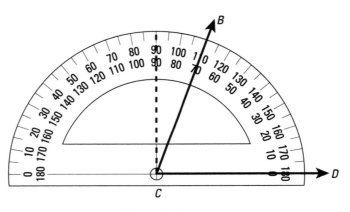

∠ BCD = 70°

  Help!

▶ An acute angle is any angle measuring less than 90°.

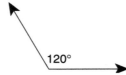
25°

▶ An obtuse angle is any angle measuring more than 90°.

120°

▶ A right angle is an angle that measures 90°.

90°

11

▶ A straight angle measures 180°.

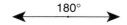

▶ A reflex angle is any angle measuring more than 180° but less than 360°.

animal offspring

Adult	Young	Adult	Young
Antelope	kid	Goose	gosling
Bear	cub	Hare	leveret
Beaver	kit	Hawk	eyas
Bird	nestling	Hog	piglet, shoat
Cat	kitten	Horse	colt
Cow	calf, heifer	Kangaroo	joey
Deer	fawn	Lion	cub
Dog	puppy, whelp	Rooster	cockerel
Dolphin	calf	Rabbit	bunny
Duck	duckling	Seal	pup. whelp
Eagle	eaglet	Shark	cub
Eel	elver	Sheep	lamb, lambkin
Elephant	calf	Swan	cygnet
Fish	fingerling	Tiger	cub
Fox	cub, kit	Turkey	poult
Giraffe	calf	Whale	calf
Goat	kid	Zebra	colt

annuity

An investment in which an amount of money is paid to the investor every year.

anonymous

Having an unknown name or a name not revealed; used when an author's name is not known. The abbreviation *anon.* is often used.

antecedent

A noun, which can be either a word or a phrase, to which a pronoun refers.

> **Example:** *Marisa* treated herself to a hot fudge sundae.

A pronoun must agree with its antecedent in person, case, and number.

See **pronoun.**

antonym A word that means the opposite of another word.

Examples:

hot	cold
love	hate
empty	full
sweet	sour
win	lose
light	dark

See also **synonym.**

apex The highest point of a geometric figure.

apex

apostrophe ['] A punctuation mark used in contractions, possessives, and some plurals of numbers, letters, and abbreviations.

Contractions

▶ Use an apostrophe to replace one or more letters or numbers that have been left out.

Examples:

do not	don't
you have	you've
1989	'89

Possessives

▶ Use an apostrophe to show that an object belongs to someone or something.

Singular Nouns

▶ Add an apostrophe and *s* to singular nouns.

Examples: Walter's book
a boy's coat
one dog's bone

▶ If a person's name or a word ends in *s,* add an apostrophe and *s.*

Examples: Chris's new car
waitress's tray

▶ When two people own one thing, add an apostrophe and *s* to the last name only.

Example: Larry and Helen's science project
(one project)

▶ When two people each own a different thing, add an apostrophe and *s* to both names.

Example: Larry's and Helen's science projects
(two projects)

Compound Words

▶ Add an apostrophe and *s* to the last word of compound words.

Examples: everybody else's
mother-in-law's home (singular)
brothers-in-law's cars (plural)

Plural Nouns

▶ Add an apostrophe and *s* to plural nouns not ending in *s*.

Examples: children's toys
deer's antlers
men's papers

▶ Add only an apostrophe to plural nouns ending with the letter *s*.

Examples: ladies' hats
boys' houses
girls' dresses

Other Plurals

▶ Add an apostrophe and *s* to a letter, a number, or an abbreviation with periods to show more than one.

Examples: five A's
two 6's
several Ph.D.'s

appendix

A section in the back of a book that gives the reader additional useful information. An appendix might include charts, diagrams, lists, maps, or tables. For example, in a literature book, the plays of Shakespeare might be listed.

Appendix I

Comedies
Love's Labor Lost
The Comedy of Errors
Two Gentlemen of Verona
A Midsummer Night's Dream
The Merchant of Venice
The Taming of the Shrew
The Merry Wives of Windsor
Much Ado About Nothing
As You Like It
Twelfth Night
All's Well That Ends Well
Measure for Measure

Tragedies
Romeo and Juliet
Titus Andronicus
Julius Caesar
Troilus and Cressida
Hamlet
Othello

King Lear
Macbeth
Timon of Athens
Antony and Cleopatra
Coriolanus

Histories
King Henry VI, Parts 1, 2, and 3
King Richard III
King Richard II
King John
King Henry IV, Parts 1 and 2
King Henry V
King Henry VIII

Romances
Pericles
Cymbeline
The Winter's Tale
The Tempest

appositive

A word or group of words that give further explanation of a noun or pronoun.

Example: Miss Pepper, *the school's cook,* uses too much salt.

Buck, *our new dog,* is a black Labrador.

arc

A part of a circle connecting the two parts of the whole circle.

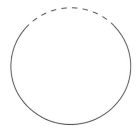

area   The number of square units inside a shape, such as a rectangle.

▶ To find the area of a rectangle, multiply the length times the width.

W = 2 feet
L = 4 feet
$A = L \times W$
A = 4 feet x 2 feet
A = 8 square feet

W = 2'   L = 4'

▶ To find the area of a square, multiply the length times width.

$A = L \times W$
A = 4 inches x 4 inches
A = 16 inches

4"
4"

▶ To find the area of a triangle, measure the base. Then measure the height. The area will equal 1/2 the base times 1/2 the height.

A = 1/2 bh (base/height)
A = 1/2 (12 inches x 6 inches)
A = 1/2 x 72
A = 36 sq. in.

6"
12"

array   An orderly arrangement of a set of objects put in rows and columns, usually rectangular in shape.

This array shows 5 groups of objects, 2 in each group, or 5 x 2 = 10.

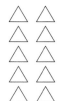

art elements	The characteristics found in art work.

Color	Space	Style
Line	Content	Composition
Texture	Subject matter	

article   A word such as *a*, *an*, or *the* used to introduce nouns and determine whether the nouns are definite (specific) or indefinite (any). Articles can act as adjectives.

▶ The word *a* is used before nouns beginning with a consonant. (indefinite)

Examples: a cat   a spoon   a fishing pole

▶ The word *an* is used before nouns beginning with vowels. (indefinite)

Example: an elephant   an ostrich   an apple

▶ The word *the* is used before nouns that refer to a specific person or item. (definite)

Examples: the girl   the train   the class

associative property   The order in which addends or factors are grouped in a problem does not change the sum (the answer in addition) or the product (the answer in multiplication).

$$5 + (4 + 6) = 15$$
$$(5 + 4) + 6 = 15$$
$$(5 \times 2) \times 4 = 10 \times 4 + 40$$
$$5 \times (2 \times 4) = 5 \times 8 = 40$$

Only addition and multiplication are associative.

asymmetric   Any design or figure that cannot be divided evenly to mirror itself.

Example: $\mathcal{G}$ The letter *g* is asymmetric because it cannot be divided to equal itself in shape and size.

See **symmetry.**

atlas | A book of maps. Use an atlas to find information about

agriculture   flags of countries   mountain ranges
areas   important industries   populations
capitals   language   religions
currency   largest cities   rivers

atmospheric layers | The four layers of the atmosphere. The lowest is the *troposphere*, above which are the *stratosphere*, *mesosphere*, and the highest, the *thermosphere*.

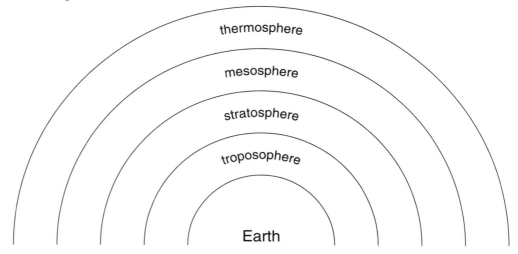

attribute | A quality or characteristic belonging to a set of figures, such as the color, size, and shape of the set.

These pyramids have common attributes. They

1. have points.
2. are three-dimensional.
3. have at least three sides.
4. have a base.

 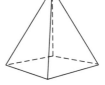 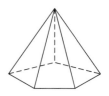

autobiography | The story of a person's life, written by the person.

average | An amount found by adding a group of numbers together and dividing the answer by the number of numerals in the group.

Example: Find the average of 4, 5, and 3.

First, add the numbers together.

$$\begin{array}{r} 4 \\ 5 \\ +\ 3 \\ \hline 12 \end{array}$$

Then, count the numbers added.

$$\begin{array}{r} 4 \\ 5 \quad \textbf{3 numbers} \\ +\ 3 \\ \hline 12 \end{array}$$

Divide the answer (12) by the number of numerals counted (3).

$$3\overline{)12} \quad \textbf{The average is 4.}$$

▶ Another name for average is *mean*.

axis | In science, an imaginary pole that runs through the middle of the earth and extends through the North Pole and South Pole.

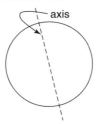

In math, the outer lines on a grid. The vertical line is called the *y* axis, and the horizontal line is the *x* axis.

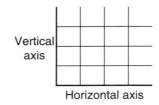

ballad

A short narrative poem that can be sung. It is written in stanzas of four lines and tells of brave deeds, love, and sadness.

The Village Blacksmith (First stanza)

Under a spreading chestnut-tree
    The village smithy stands;
The smith, a mighty man is he,
    With large and sinewy hands;
And the muscles of his brawny arms
    Are strong as iron bands.

    —Henry Wadsworth Longfellow

bank check

A written order to a bank to pay money from an account to a person, business, or organization.

Writing a Check

John J. Doe 123 Main St. Hometown, State, Zip Code	001 Date _____
Pay to the Order of_____	$ _____
_____ Dollars	
1st National Bank of USA	
Memo _____	_____

▶ Write a date on the check.

▶ Write the name of the person or business receiving the check.

▶ Write in the dollar and cents amount in words. Draw a line in the leftover space.

▶ Write in the dollars and cents in numerals as close as possible to the dollar sign.

▶ Sign the check, writing your name as it appears at the bank.

Endorsing a Check

```
Endorse here
```

▶ Endorsing a check means signing the back of a check that has been paid to you so that you can deposit it in your bank account.

▶ Write your signature on the *back* side of the check exactly as it appears on the front side. Use the space provided.

bar graph   *See* **graph.**

base word   A word without a prefix or a suffix. A base word is sometimes called a "root word."

Examples:

Prefix	Base Word	Suffix
un	happy	
	pick	ing
dis	appear	ance

B. C.   An abbreviation meaning the time in years before the birth of Christ.

Example: The date 776 B.C. means seven hundred seventy-six years before the birth of Christ.

B.C. is placed *after* the date.   2000 B.C.

A.D. is placed *before* the date.   A.D. 1934

Dates written without letters are assumed to be A.D.

William J. Clinton became president in 1993.

A.D. and B.C. are used *after* centuries written as words.

fourteenth century A.D.

fourth century B.C.

See also **A. D.**

B.C.E.   An abbreviation meaning before the Christian or common era. Used the same way as B.C.

bedrock   The layer of rock beneath the soil.

bibliography   A list of books and other written works arranged in alphabetical order by author. The bibliography is found at the end of a book or a school paper. Some of the books and articles were used by the author, and all contain more information about topics discussed by the author.

▶ List the author's last name first and then the first name or initials.

▶ List the title of the book, magazine, or other publication.

▶ List where the book or work was published.

▶ List the publisher.

▶ List the year of publication.

Examples:

Article: Write the author's name.

Write the title of the article in quotation marks.

Write the name of the magazine in italics.

Write the date of the issue of the magazine. Write the pages where the information was found.

Churchman, Deborah. "Bashers, Furry Fliers, and Other Ancient
Wonders." *Ranger Rick,* January 1996, pp. 34–37.

Book: Write the author's name.

Write the title of the book in italics.

Write the city and the name of the publisher.

Write the date of publication.

Andrews, Ray. *All About Dinosaurs.* New York: Random House, 1963.

Encyclopedia: Write the author's name.

Write the title of the article in quotation marks.

Write the name of the encyclopedia in italics.

Write the date of publication.

Crystal, David. "Dinosaur." *The Cambridge Encyclopedia,* 1990.

▶ Remember to list the sources in alphabetical order by author
whether it is a book, article, or other source.

Bill of Rights   The first ten amendments to the U.S. Constitution, which list the rights
guaranteed to every American citizen.

Amendments:

1. Religious and political freedom, including freedom of speech
2. Right to keep and bear arms
3. Limited quartering of soldiers
4. Freedom from unreasonable search and seizure
5. Due process of law
6. Rights of the accused
7. Right to jury trial
8. Freedom from excessive bail and punishment
9. Other rights not specifically named
10. Rights of the states and the people

biography   A story written about someone's life.

blend | Two or three consonants sounded together, so that each one can be heard. A blend is sometimes called a consonant cluster.

Examples:

bl	*bl*ock	gl	*gl*ad	spr	*spr*ing
br	*br*ing	gr	*gr*ass	st	*st*op
cl	*cl*ay	pl	*pl*an	str	*str*eet
cr	*cr*eep	pr	*pr*ince	sw	*sw*ing
dr	*dr*ink	sm	*sm*all	tr	*tr*ain
fl	*fl*ag	sn	*sn*ap	tw	*tw*in
fr	*fr*om	sp	*sp*ank		

book parts | The parts of a book include the following:

Title page: The title page names the title of the book, the author's name, the illustrator's name, and the name of the publisher.

Copyright page: The copyright page is found on the reverse side of the title page. It includes the year the book was published, the publisher's name, and the ISBN number of the book. ISBN is an abbreviation for International Standard Book Number, a ten-digit identification number given to all books when they are published. The copyright symbol © indicates that only the author and/or the publisher has the legal rights to the book.

Dedication page: Sometimes an author dedicates the book to a special person or persons. Not all books have a dedication page.

Table of contents: This is a listing of all the chapters and their page numbers.

Body: The main section of a book.

Author/illustrator page: This page gives information about the author and illustrator. Sometimes this information is found on the book jacket or on the back cover of the book.

Bibliography: A bibliography lists books and other written sources that the author used as references in writing the book. It may also include a list of books recommended for further reading.

See **bibliography.**

Index: Located at the back of a book, an index lists alphabetically all subjects contained in the book and the pages on which they can be found.

See **index.**

book report   A summary of the most important events or ideas found in a book; also, comments about the book.

▶ Tell what kind of story you are reporting about: adventure, humor, mystery, western, history, or other.

▶ Tell only the most important ideas or events, not the details.

▶ Never tell the conclusion of the story.

Guide Questions

1. Have you told what kind of story it is and where it takes place?
2. Have you told who the main character is?
3. Have you told what the main character did or needed to do?
4. Have you told what problem the main character had?
5. Have you given a clue to the solution of the problem without telling the ending?
6. Did you like the book?

Example:

Title: *The Story of Ferdinand*

Author: Munro Leaf

Illustrator: Robert Lawson

Main Characters: Ferdinand, his mother, and men from Madrid

Plot Summary: This is an adventure story about Ferdinand, a bull who grew up in Spain. Unlike most bulls who loved to bump heads and fight, Ferdinand liked to sit quietly and smell the flowers. His mother worried about him. One day, because he was the biggest and strongest bull in the pasture, men from Madrid came to the field and took Ferdinand to Madrid to fight in the bull ring. There he had a most unusual experience.

borrowing | In subtraction, the process of exchanging or regrouping numbers to the next smaller place value.

1. Begin at the ones place: 7 cannot be subtracted from 4.

        5 tens 4 ones   5 4
      – 2 tens 7 ones   – 2 7

2. Since they are equal in value, rename or exchange the 5 tens as 4 tens and 10 ones. Add the 10 ones with the 4 ones already there. There are now 14 ones. Now subtract 7 ones from 14 ones. Write the difference in the ones column.

        4 tens 14 ones   4 14
        5̶ tens 4̶ ones   5̶4̶
      – 2 tens   7 ones   – 2 7
               7 ones   7

3. Draw a slash through the 5 in the tens column and write a 4 above it to show 1 ten has been borrowed or exchanged and 4 tens remain.

        4 tens 14 ones   4 14
        5̶ tens 4̶ ones   5̶4̶
      – 2 tens   7 ones   – 2 7
        2 tens   7 ones   2 7

4. Next, subtract 2 tens from the 4 tens.

               14   4 14
        5 tens 4̶ ones   5̶4̶
      – 2 tens   7 ones   – 2 7
        2 tens   7 ones   2 7

Subtracting from the tens place is done in the same way, except you will be exchanging or regrouping from the hundreds place.

1. Take 1 hundred from the 7 hundreds and exchange it for 10 tens.

2. Place the 10 tens next to the 2 tens.

   10 tens + 2 tens = 12 tens

3. Now you can subtract 4 tens from 12 tens.

4. To finish the problem, subtract 3 hundred from the 6 hundreds.

$$
\begin{array}{r}
{\scriptstyle 6\ 12} \\
7\!\!\!/2\,6 \\
-\ 3\,4\,2 \\
\hline
3\,8\,4
\end{array}
$$

B. P.   An abbreviation meaning "before the present time." Used in the same manner as B.C.

brackets   Symbols that group together numbers to make equations easier to read.

▶ Use brackets when it is necessary to use a set of parentheses within parentheses.

   Example: 2 [a + 2b (3 + c)]

▶ Brackets are also used to insert an explanation or correction into quoted material.

   Example: The narrator commented, "He [Neil Armstrong] was the first man to walk on the moon."

business letter   *See* **letter writing.**

cabinet   A group of fourteen members chosen by the president to head the executive departments of the government and to serve as advisers to the president. The cabinet members are the heads of the departments of state, treasury, defense, justice, agriculture, interior, commerce, labor, health and human services, housing and urban development, energy, education, transportation, and veterans affairs.

calculator

An instrument used to solve mathematical problems, such as those dealing with addition, subtraction, multiplication, division, percentages, and square root.

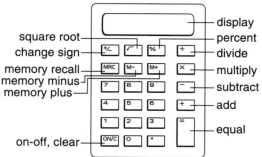

Basic Key Functions

C	clear/correction
M+	addition to the number in the memory
M-	subtraction from the number in the memory
MR/C	to recall or cancel from the memory

calendar

A chart showing the days, weeks, and months of a year.

Days of the Week

There are seven days in a week.

Day	Abbreviation
Sunday	Sun.
Monday	Mon.
Tuesday	Tues.
Wednesday	Wed.
Thursday	Thurs.
Friday	Fri.
Saturday	Sat.

Months

There are twelve months in a year.

Month	Abbreviation	Days
January	Jan.	31
February	Feb.	28 (29 in a leap year)
March	Mar.	31
April	Apr.	30
May	May	31
June	June	30
July	July	31
August	Aug.	31
September	Sept.	30
October	Oct.	31
November	Nov.	30
December	Dec.	31

An easy way to remember the number of days in each month:

1. Make a fist.
2. Touch the knuckle of your first finger and call it "January." It has 31 days.
3. Touch the space between your first knuckle and second knuckle. Call this "February." It has 28 days.
4. While saying the months of the year in order, every "knuckle month" will have 31 days. Every "space" month will have 30 days, except February, which has 28.
5. After July, begin again with "August" on your first knuckle.

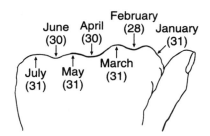

Years

365 days	=	1 year
366 days	=	1 leap year
52 weeks	=	1 year
12 months	=	1 year
10 years	=	1 decade
100 years	=	1 century

▶ A leap year occurs every four years; 1992 and 1996 were leap years.

How to write the date:

November 12, 1997
Nov. 12, 1997
11/12/97

can/may

The word *can* is an auxiliary (helping) verb, meaning someone has the knowledge or skill to do something.

Example: You *can* save money by buying that bike on sale.

The word *may* is an auxiliary verb used to ask permission to do something.

Example: *May* I help carry your packages?

capacity

See **measurement.**

capital

In finance, money and property used by a business to transact its trade.

capital letter

A letter written or printed in a larger size and sometimes in a different form than the lower-case version.

▶ Capitalize the first word in a sentence.

Example: Please feed the baby.

▶ Capitalize the first word in every line of poetry.

Examples: A new capital every time
You begin a new line of rhyme.

▶ Capitalize the first word in a direct quotation.

Examples: The clown asked, "Are you having fun?"
"Yes, I am," answered the boy.

▶ Capitalize the names and initials of persons.

Examples: James Tyler Smith
J. T. Smith
Patricia R. Penny
P. R. Penny

▶ Capitalize titles of persons that come before the names.

Examples: President Wilson
Captain Anderson
Senator Lawson
Bishop Cartwright

▶ Do not capitalize titles that follow names.

Examples: John Anderson, a captain in the Marines
Mary Clark, president of CRC

▶ Capitalize abbreviations of titles and names.

Examples: Dr. Black
Gen. McArthur
Sam Standish, Sr.
John Johnson, Jr.

▶ Many abbreviations do not require capitals.

Examples: doz.
in.
ft
yd
vol

▶ Capitalize words that show a family relationship when they are used as names or with the person's given name.

Examples: Will Mother be late, Sis?

I wrote a note to Aunt Marcy.

But: My mother is late.

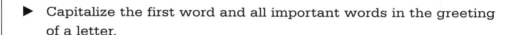

▶ Capitalize days of the week, months of the year, and names of holidays.

Examples: Monday, Tuesday

January, February

Thanksgiving, Christmas

▶ Seasons of the year should not be capitalized.

Examples: spring

summer

fall

winter

▶ Capitalize the first word and all important words in the greeting of a letter.

Examples: Hi, Dad,

Dear Aunt Jo and Uncle Cal,

▶ Capitalize the first word in the closing of a letter.

Examples: Sincerely yours,

Very truly yours,

Your friend,

▶ Capitalize names of races, nationalities, tribes, languages, and religions.

Examples: Apache

French

German

Jewish

▶ Do not capitalize words based on size or color.

Examples: thin man, tall woman

▶ Capitalize words naming special places.

Examples: Grand Canyon
South Dakota
Atlantic Ocean
the Northeast

▶ Capitalize words like *northeast* only when they are used as a location and not a direction.

Examples: Andy lives in the Northeast. (location)
Amy traveled northeast. (direction)

▶ Capitalize names of organizations and businesses.

Examples: the Democratic Party
Chicago Symphony Orchestra
Boy Scouts of America
the Ford Motor Company

▶ Capitalize names of school subjects that are names of languages or used as titles.

Examples: English
Latin
Spelling
Algebra

▶ Names of school subjects used as part of a sentence are not capitalized unless they are names of languages.

Examples: Lola has gym at 11 o'clock.
Sandy is studying English.

▶ Capitalize the first and important words in titles of books, magazines, newspapers, or other works.

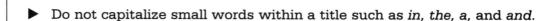

Examples: The *Chicago Tribune*
The Case of the Lost Jewel

▶ Do not capitalize small words within a title such as *in, the, a,* and *and.*

▶ Capitalize names of historic events and documents.

Examples: the Bill of Rights
the Civil War

▶ Capitalize abbreviations of historical times and organizations, businesses, and departments in government.

| A.D. | B.C. | IRS | WWII |
| CBS | NATO | IBM | YMCA |

▶ Always capitalize the word *I.*

Examples: I finished my work.
When I finish, I can go swimming.

cardinal number

A number that shows *how many.*

Examples: 429
1
23

See also **ordinal number.**

carrying | In addition, the process of regrouping numbers to the next larger place value.

1. Begin at the ones place: Add 8 and 6 together. They equal 14.

       5 tens   8 ones   **58**
     + 3 tens   6 ones   **+ 36**
       8 tens   14 ones   **94**

2. Since they are equal in value, rename the 14 ones as 1 ten and 4 ones. Write the 4 in the ones column and add or carry the 1 ten to the numbers in the tens column.

       1 ten   1
       5 tens   8 ones   **58**
     + 3 tens   6 ones   **+ 36**
                4 ones   **4**

3. Add the digits in the tens column, including the 1 ten that was carried.

       1 ten   1
       5 tens   8 ones   **58**
     − 3 tens   6 ones   **+ 36**
       9 tens   4 ones   **94**

Carrying or adding three-digit or larger numbers would be done in the same way, always regrouping, carrying, and renaming to the next larger place value.

                                            1 1
     3 hundreds   6 tens   7 ones   **367**
   + 5 hundreds   4 tens   7 ones   **+ 547**
     8 hundreds   10 tens   14 ones   **914**

casting out nines | A method of checking the accuracy of an addition, subtraction, multiplication, or division problem.

Addition

Example: **End Digits**

$$236 = 2 + 3 + 6 = 11 - 9 = 2$$
$$327 = 3 + 2 + 7 = 12 - 9 = 3$$
$$+\ 158 = 1 + 5 + 8 = 14 - 9 = 5$$
$$721$$

Add the end digits and subtract 9 from the total.

$$2$$
$$3$$
$$+\ 5$$
$$10 - 9 = ①$$

Add the numbers in the sum; subtract 9 from the total.

$$721 = 7 + 2 + 1 = 10 - 9 = ①$$

When each casting out process ends up with the same number, the problem has been added correctly.

Subtraction

The same process is used in casting out nines in subtraction as in addition, except that the end digits are subtracted.

Example: **End Digits**

$$756 = 7 + 5 + 6 = 18 - 9 = \quad 9$$
$$-\ 29 = 2 + 9 \qquad = 11 - 9 = -\ 2$$
$$727 \qquad\qquad\qquad\qquad\qquad\qquad ⑦$$

$$727 = 7 + 2 + 7 = 16 - 9 = \quad ⑦$$

Multiplication

The same process is used except that the two end digits are multiplied.

    Example: **End Digits**

$$463 = 4 + 6 + 3 = 13 - 9 = \quad 4$$
$$\underline{\times\ 37} = 3 + 7 \qquad = 10 - 9 = \underline{\times\ 1}$$
$$3241 \qquad\qquad\qquad\qquad\qquad ④$$
$$\underline{1389}$$
$$17131 \quad = 1 + 7 + 1 + 3 + 1 = 13 - 9 = ④$$

Long Division

Divide the problem in the usual way.

    Example:

$$\begin{array}{r} 28 \\ 24\overline{\smash{)}672} \\ \underline{48} \\ 192 \\ \underline{192} \end{array}$$

Then, follow these steps to check your answer:

Multiply the quotient by the divisor.

$$\begin{array}{r} 28 \\ \underline{\times\ 24} \\ 112 \\ \underline{56} \\ 672 \end{array}$$

Cast out nines as in multiplication problems.

    Example: **End Digits**

$$28 = 2 + 8 = 10 - 9 = \quad 1$$
$$\underline{\times\ 24} = 2 + 4 = 6 \qquad = \underline{\times\ 6}$$
$$112 \qquad\qquad\qquad\qquad ⑥$$
$$\underline{56}$$
$$672 = 6 + 7 + 2 = 15 - 9 = ⑥$$

Celsius thermometer

A metric thermometer named for its inventor, Anders Celsius (it is also known as a centigrade thermometer). On the Celsius thermometer scale, 0 degrees is the temperature at which water freezes, and 100 degrees is the temperature at which water boils.

The temperature 8°C is read as "eight degrees Celsius."

To convert a Celsius temperature to a Fahrenheit temperature, multiply the Celsius temperature by 9, divide by 5, and add 32.

Formula:
(Celsius temp. x 9) ÷ 5 + 32° = Fahrenheit temp.

Example:
(10°C x 9) ÷ 5 = 18 + 32° = 50°F.

See also **Fahrenheit thermometer.**

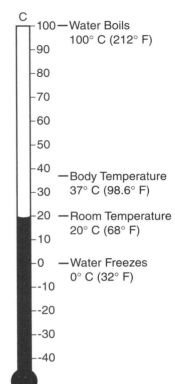

C
- 100 — Water Boils 100° C (212° F)
- 90
- 80
- 70
- 60
- 50
- 40 — Body Temperature 37° C (98.6° F)
- 30
- 20 — Room Temperature 20° C (68° F)
- 10
- 0 — Water Freezes 0° C (32° F)
- -10
- -20
- -30
- -40

centimeter

A unit of length in the metric system equal to 1/100 of a meter. Use a centimeter ruler to measure short lengths.

10 millimeters (mm)	=	1 centimeter (cm)
10 centimeters (cm)	=	1 decimeter (dm)
100 millimeters (mm)	=	1 decimeter (dm)
10 decimeters (dm)	=	1 meter (m)
100 centimeters (cm)	=	1 meter (m)
1000 meters (m)	=	1 kilometer (km)

See also **measurement.**

chord A straight line connecting any two points on the circumference of a circle or a closed curve.

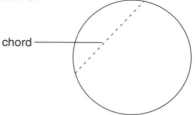

chord —

cinquain A five-line stanza with a set number of syllables in each line. Invented by Adelaide Crapsey, who was greatly influenced by Japanese haiku.

— — (two syllables)
— — — — (four syllables)
— — — — — — (six syllables)
— — — — — — — — (eight syllables)
— — (two syllables)

Example:

Kitten
Soft and fluffy
Sleeps, yawns, stretches, and purrs
Makes me feel warm, cozy, happy
Nice pet.

circle *See* **geometric figures.**

circumference The curved line of a circle; the length around a circle. The circumference of a circle is a little more than three times its diameter. (The diameter is a straight line through the center of the circle from one point on the circle to the opposite point on the circle.)

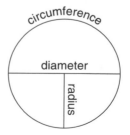

circumference

diameter

radius

Help!

To find the circumference of a circle:

▶ Measure the diameter.

▶ Multiply the diameter by 3.14 (which is known as pi).

▶ Or, for a quick estimate of a circumference, multiply the diameter by 3.

Example: Diameter = 4 inches   Then 4 x 3 = 12 inches

The circumference measures about 12 inches.

See also **diameter** *and* **pi.**

clause

A group of words containing a verb (action word) and a subject. A clause may be a complete sentence or part of a sentence.

Independent clause: Contains a subject and predicate and makes sense by itself.

Example: Although it rained every day, <u>Joe enjoyed his vacation.</u>

Dependent clause: Contains a subject and predicate but does not make sense by itself. It needs an independent clause to make sense.

Example: I ducked <u>when Sam threw the ball.</u>

▶ Some words can be used to connect dependent, or subordinate, clauses with independent or main clauses.

after, although, as, because, before, how, though, unless, until, when, where, while

clef | A symbol placed on a musical staff to indicate the names and pitches of notes.

Treble clef:

▶ High notes are placed on the treble clef.

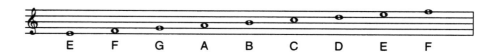

E F G A B C D E F

▶ Lines named on the treble staff are

E G B D F
Every **G**ood **B**oy **D**oes **F**ine

▶ Spaces named on the treble staff are

F A C E
The letters spell FACE.

Bass clef:

▶ Lower notes are placed on the bass clef.

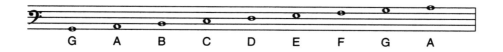

G A B C D E F G A

▶ Lines named on the bass clef are

G B D F A
Good **B**oys **D**on't **F**ool **A**round

▶ Spaces named on the bass clef are

A C E G
All **C**ows **E**at **G**rass

Also see **staff.**

cliché | An expression that has been overused and has become commonplace.

Example: You *can't teach an old dog new tricks.*
My desk is *clean as a whistle.*

closed figure | A geometric figure that begins and ends at the same point.

clouds | White, gray, or dark gray shapes made up of tiny water droplets of water or ice crystals.

Type	Characteristics	Form	Altitude
altocumulus	white, gray, puffy, layered, fleecy	ice crystals	2–6 miles
altostratus	white, gray sheet, bluish	water droplets ice crystals	2–6 miles
cirrocumulus	thin, puffy, rippled	ice crystals	5–9 miles
cirrostratus	thin sheet, hazy, halos the sun	ice crystals	6 miles
cirrus	thin, wispy	ice crystals	7–12 miles
cumulonimbus	dark storm cloud, produces heavy rain, thunder, hail	water droplets ice crystals	4–6 miles
cumulus	large, white, puffy, dense, flat base	water droplets	2 miles
nimbostratus	dark; rain, sleet, or snow falls from it	water droplets	1/4 mile
stratocumulus	white with gray patches, horizontal layers, rounded tops	water droplets rainfall; fog	1 mile
stratus	flat, gray horizontal	layer of fog	1 mile

clustering | A method of organizing thoughts before writing about a topic.

See **webbing.**

colon [:] | A punctuation mark used to introduce an explanation or a list. A colon is also used with numerals to show time and in the greeting of a business letter.

Examples: The color of her dress is violet:
a beautiful bluish purple. (explanation)
Please bring the following items to class:
pencils, paper, and rulers. (list)
3:30 p.m. (time)
Dear Sir: (greeting)
Dear Mrs. Blake: (greeting)

Colonies | The original 13 states of the United States. They are New Hampshire, Massachusetts, Rhode Island, Connecticut, New York, New Jersey, Pennsylvania, Delaware, Maryland, Virginia, North Carolina, South Carolina, and Georgia.

See **United States of America.**

comma [,] | A punctuation mark placed where a pause in speaking would be made.

▶ Address: Use a comma as part of an address.

Examples: Her address is 123 Oak Street, Chicago, IL 60610.
Tom lives on Rural Route 2, Ames, IA 50010.
You can send Jane's letter to Apt. 728, 114 Elm Street, Dallas, TX 75206.
Send your request to Box 123, Cleveland, OH 44115.

▶ City in state or county: Use a comma to separate the name of a city from the state or country.

Examples: Kevin lives in Arlington, Virginia.
London, England, is an important city in Europe.
We visited Disney World in Orlando, Florida.

▶ Conjunctions: Use a comma between two independent clauses joined by the conjunctions *and, but, or, for, nor, so,* or *yet.*

Examples: Tom hit a long fly ball, and Joe scored the winning run.
It rained all day, but the ballgame was played.
Help me with this work, or I'll never finish.

▶ Conjunctive adverbs: Use a comma after conjunctive adverbs such as *however, nevertheless, therefore,* and *furthermore.*

Example: I read the book; however, I didn't like the ending.

▶ Dates: Use a comma after parts of a date.

Examples: She was born on July 28, 1994.
We moved to Dallas on May 11, 1996.
School began on September 5, 1997, and ended on
June 10, 1998.
Today is Tuesday, January 30, 1999.

▶ Do not use a comma between a month and a year.

Example: December 1899.

▶ Direct address: Use a comma when you are speaking directly to someone.

Examples: Sandy, please help me.
What will you wear to the dance, Sally?
Hurry, Sue, or we'll be late.
Connor, will you bake some cookies?

▶ Direct quotation: Use a comma before or after a direct quotation.

Examples: "Mom, I won the race," called Andy.
Juanita sighed, "I have to clean my room."

▶ Letters Use a comma after the greeting of a friendly letter.

Examples: Dear Tina,
Dear Mr. Smith,

Also use a comma after the closing of all letters.

Examples: Your friend,
Sincerely yours,

▶ Parenthetical expressions: Use a comma before and after parenthetical expressions, such as *by the way, for example,* or *on the other hand.*

Example: The baseball team, for example, always rides in a special bus.

▶ Series: Use a comma to separate items in a list in a sentence.

Examples: Paul enjoys watching baseball, football, and tennis.
The winning numbers were 43, 2, 70, and 100.
I looked for my keys under the bed, in the drawer, and in my purse.
When boating, wear a life jacket, carry a flashlight, take fresh water, and stay with your group.

▶ Too: Use a comma to separate the word *too* in a sentence.

Examples: Phil likes to play tennis, too.
August, too, is a hot month.

▶ Yes, no, well, oh: Use a comma after *yes, no, well,* and *oh* when they begin sentences.

Examples: Yes, I'll be ready at noon.
No, lunch isn't ready.
Well, what will we do now?
Oh, I can't wait for the circus to come!

common factor

Any factors that two numbers have in common.

Examples: The bold print indicates the factors that 24 and 32 have in common.
Factors for 24 : **1,2**,3,**4**,6,**8**,12,24
Factors for 32 : **1,2,4,8**,16,32

The largest number that 24 and 32 have in common is 8. It is called the greatest common factor (GFC).

commutative property

The order of the addends does not change the sum.

5 + 6 = 11   6 + 5 = 11   addition

The order of the factors does not change the product.

8 x 3 = 24   3 x 8 = 24   multiplication

compass rose

A symbol printed on a chart or map to show the points of a compass, numbered from true north and showing 360°.

▶ Memorizing "Never Eat Soggy Waffles" (North, East, South, West) will help you remember the directions in order.

complementary angle	Any of two angles that add up to 90 degrees.

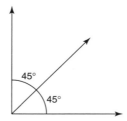

45°
45°

compound interest	Interest earned on an original sum of money plus interest earned on the interest.

compound sentence	A sentence with two or more complete thoughts (independent clauses) joined together by words that connect, called conjunctions *(and, but, or, nor, for, yet,* and *so).*

    Example: Tim came early, and we went to the zoo.
                (Each complete thought could be a sentence by itself.)

▶ Use a comma before the conjunction to separate the two parts of the sentence.

compound subject	Two or more simple subjects (nouns or pronouns) that share the same predicate.

    Example: Tom and Ron played tennis.
                Carol and I like pizza.

compound word

Two words combined or put together to form one word.

Examples: butter + fly   butterfly
play + ground   playground

Common Compound Words

anyone	headline	quarterback
blackboard	indoor	railroad
classroom	lightweight	sidewalk
downstairs	mailman	themselves
everywhere	northeast	underwear
flashlight	outdoor	weekend
grandfather	paperback	yourself

▶ Common compound words that need hyphens:

cave-in	father-in-law	merry-go-round
do-it-yourself	flea-bitten	old-fashioned
drive-in	great-grandfather	person-to-person
editor-in-chief	jack-in-the-box	self-confident

computer words

Address: Letters or numbers that tell a computer where to find information.

Backup: A copy of a disk, program, or file.

Basic: A simple computer programming language.

Binary code: A system using only 1 and 0 in different combinations to represent letters, numbers, and characters.

Bug: An error or problem in a computer program.

CD-ROM: An abbreviated name for compact disk-read only memory, capable of storing large amounts of information.

Command: An order that tells a computer what to do, given by pressing one or more keys on the keyboard.

Computer: A piece of hardware that takes in information, processes and stores it, and prints it out.

CPU: Central processing unit, the control center of a computer.

Crash: The breakdown of a computer program or of the computer itself.

Cursor: A symbol that shows where the next letter, number, or mark will appear on the video screen.

Data: Information given to, stored in, or processed by a computer.

Data bank: Information stored in a computer's memory.

Default: A preset or automatic action the computer system chooses unless the user gives it a different order.

Disk: A device used to store large amounts of information to be used by a computer.

Document: Information created and put on a disk or file.

Eject: to remove a disk from a disk drive.

File: A collection of information, such as an application program or a document stored on disk.

Floppy disk: A plastic disk capable of storing computer information.

Font: A collection of letters and numbers in different sizes and designs.

Graphic: A picture made by a computer.

Hardware: Computer equipment, including the keyboard, video monitor, printer, disks, and tapes.

Input: Data given to a computer.

Keyboard: A set of keys similar to those found on a typewriter used to type information into a computer.

Loop: A part of a computer program that repeats.

Memory: An area within a computer in which information is stored.

Menu: A screen display that lists programs in the computer.

Printer: A piece of hardware that prints out information from a computer.

Program: Instructions coded to tell a computer what to do.

RAM: Random access memory, where information is stored in the computer temporarily and where information can be written or read before it is saved on a disk.

ROM: Read only memory, where information is stored in a computer on a permanent basis.

Run: A command that tells a computer to run a program it has stored in its memory.

Software: A variety of computer programs.

VDU: Visual display unit, the screen used to display computer information.

Word processor: Software that allows the user to type, edit, and finalize articles, books, and written work on an automatic typewriter or on a computer.

concave | Curved inward, like the inside surface of a bowl.

concentric circles | Circles that share the same center. A target is made up of concentric circles.

congruent figures   Figures having the same size and shape.

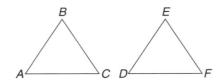

Triangles *ABC* and *DEF* are congruent triangles.

conjunction   A word that connects two or more independent clauses or complete thoughts.

> **Example:**   Dad will come to the ballgame, *but* he may be late.

Coordinating conjunction: A conjunction that joins words or phrases of equal rank.
and, but, for, nor, or, so, yet
Ken's project was well done, but it was turned in late.

Correlative conjunction: A conjunction that is used in pairs.
either/or   neither/nor   both/and
not only/but also
Neither Carol *nor* Charlene can play on Friday.

Subordinating conjunction: A conjunction that joins a dependent clause to the main part of the sentence to make a complex sentence.

after	because	so that	whenever
although	before	than	where
as	if	unless	wherever
as if	in order	until	while
as though	since	when	why

Unless you hurry, we'll miss the train.

See also **comma.**

consonant   Any letter of the alphabet that is not a vowel.

b c d f g h j k l m n p q r s t v w x y z

consonant cluster | *See* **blend.**

constellation | Any of 88 groups of the brightest stars that are thought to resemble objects, animals, and characters from mythology.

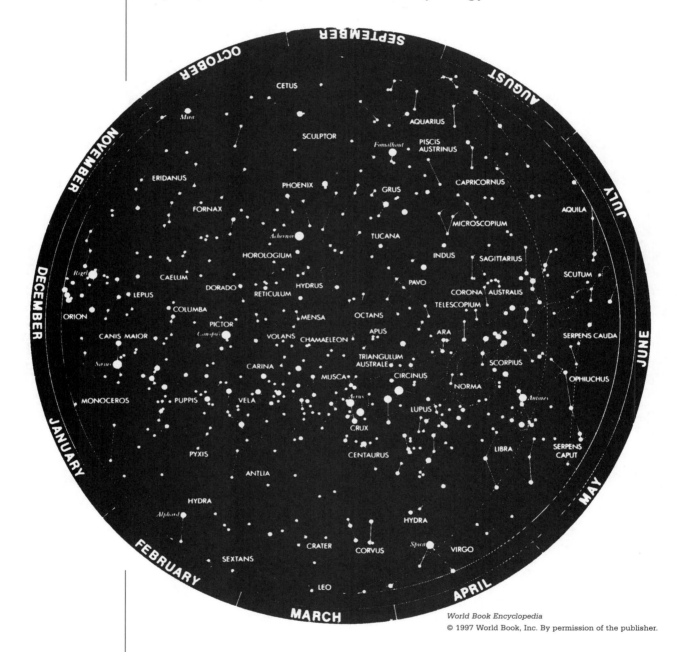

SEPTEMBER
OCTOBER
AUGUST
NOVEMBER
JULY
DECEMBER
JUNE
JANUARY
MAY
FEBRUARY
APRIL
MARCH

CETUS
Mira
AQUARIUS
SCULPTOR
Fomalhaut
PISCIS AUSTRINUS
ERIDANUS
CAPRICORNUS
PHOENIX
GRUS
AQUILA
FORNAX
MICROSCOPIUM
Achernar
TUCANA
HOROLOGIUM
INDUS
SAGITTARIUS
Rigel
CAELUM
HYDRUS
PAVO
SCUTUM
LEPUS
DORADO
RETICULUM
CORONA AUSTRALIS
COLUMBA
MENSA
OCTANS
TELESCOPIUM
ORION
PICTOR
Canopus
VOLANS
CHAMAELEON
APUS
ARA
SERPENS CAUDA
CANIS MAIOR
TRIANGULUM AUSTRALE
CARINA
SCORPIUS
Sirius
MUSCA
CIRCINUS
NORMA
OPHIUCHUS
MONOCEROS
PUPPIS
VELA
Acrux
LUPUS
Antares
CRUX
PYXIS
CENTAURUS
LIBRA
SERPENS CAPUT
ANTLIA
HYDRA
HYDRA
Alphard
Spica
CRATER
CORVUS
VIRGO
SEXTANS
LEO

World Book Encyclopedia
© 1997 World Book, Inc. By permission of the publisher.

continent | One of seven land masses of the earth: Africa, Antarctica, Asia, Australia, Europe, North America, and South America.

See also the **map of continents** *on the following page.*

continent

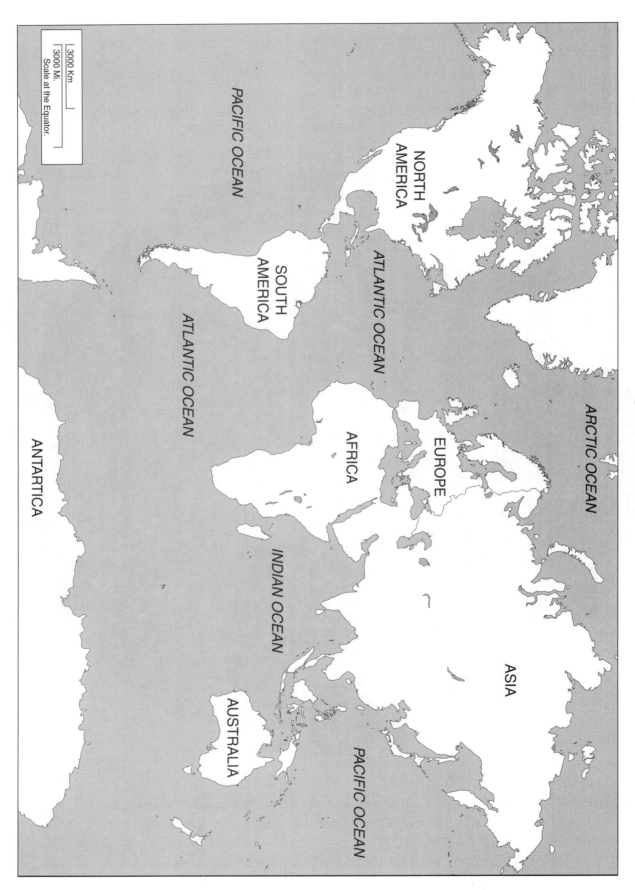

Map of Continents

PACIFIC OCEAN

NORTH
AMERICA

SOUTH
AMERICA

ATLANTIC OCEAN

ATLANTIC OCEAN

ANTARTICA

AFRICA

EUROPE

ARCTIC OCEAN

INDIAN OCEAN

ASIA

AUSTRALIA

PACIFIC OCEAN

3000 Km
3000 Mi.
Scale at the Equator.

contraction

A shortened form of two words. In a contraction, one or more letters are omitted in making the new word, and an apostrophe (') is used in place of the letter or letters that were dropped.

Common Contractions

I am	*I'm*	who is	*who's*
you are	*you're*	is not	*isn't*
it is	*it's*	are not	*aren't*
they are	*they're*	was not	*wasn't*
I have	*I've*	has not	*hasn't*
they have	*they've*	cannot	*can't*
I had	*I'd*	will not	*won't*
I will	*I'll*	does not	*doesn't*
we will	*we'll*	do not	*don't*
I would	*I'd*	did not	*didn't*
here is	*here's*	would not	*wouldn't*
there is	*there's*	should not	*shouldn't*

convex

Curving outward like the outside of a baseball cap.

coordinates

Numbers and letters that fix a point on a graph.

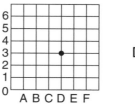

D,3

See **ordered pair.**

core

See **Earth's layer.**

counter-clockwise

A movement opposite to the direction of the hands of a clock.

counterclockwise

clockwise

court system

Federal and state courts formed to hear and settle legal disputes concerning civil, criminal, and constitutional matters.

See **United States court system.**

crust

See **Earth's layers.**

days of the week

See **calendar.**

decimal

Any base-ten numeral that uses place value to represent a number. The position of the decimal point (written as a dot) determines the value of each number.

▶ Numbers to the left of a decimal point are whole numbers called integers.

Examples: The number 7.0 is read "seven."
The number 48.0 is read "forty-eight."

▶ Numbers to the right of a decimal point are decimal fractions. Their value is less than one.

Examples: The number 0.5 is read "five-tenths."
The number 48.5 is read "forty-eight and five-tenths."

100,000,000	hundred-thousands
10,000	ten-thousands
1,000	thousands
100	hundreds
10	tens
1	ones
.	decimal point
$\frac{1}{10}$	tenths
$\frac{1}{100}$	hundredthd
$\frac{1}{1,000}$	thousandths
$\frac{1}{10,000}$	ten-thousandths
$\frac{1}{100,000}$	hundred-thousandths
$\frac{1}{1,000,000,000}$	millionths

PLACE OF DIGIT	HOW TO WRITE IT	HOW TO READ IT	FRACTION
First decimal place	.3	Three tenths	$\frac{3}{10}$
Second decimal place	.03	Three hundreths	$\frac{3}{100}$
Third decimal place	.003	Three thousandths	$\frac{3}{1000}$
Fourth decimal place	.0003	Three ten-thounsandths	$\frac{3}{10,000}$
Fifth decimal place	.00003	Three hundred-thousandths	$\frac{3}{100,000}$
Sixth decimal place	.000003	Three millionths	$\frac{3}{1,000,000,000}$

Example: 502.062 is read "five hundred two and sixty-two thousandths"

To change a decimal to a fraction, take away the decimal point, and write the number as a fraction by indicating its place value.

> **Example:** 0.25 reads "twenty-five hundredths."
> Written as a fraction, it would be 25/100
> Reduced to its lowest terms 25/100 = 1/4

To change a fraction to a decimal, divide the numerator by the denominator (bottom number) and write the quotient (answer) in decimal form as indicated by its place value.

> **Example:** to change 3/4 to a decimal

$$
\begin{array}{r}
0.75 \\
4\overline{)3.00} \\
\underline{2\,8\downarrow} \\
20 \\
\underline{20}
\end{array}
\qquad .75
$$

Be sure the position of the decimals are in line.

To add or subtract decimals:

▶ Add or subtract decimals as you would any addition or subtraction problem. The decimal points of all numbers must be in line.

▶ Fill in with zeros to the right of the decimal point if one of the numbers to be added or subtracted is shorter.

> **Example:**
>
> $$
> \begin{array}{r}
> 47.364 \\
> +\,44.220 \\
> \hline
> 91.584
> \end{array}
> \qquad
> \begin{array}{r}
> 731.500 \\
> -\,312.765 \\
> \hline
> 418.735
> \end{array}
> $$

To multiply decimals:

▶ Multiply as you would any multiplication problem.

▶ Count the places to the right of the decimal point in the problem.

▶ The number of places in the product (answer) should equal the same number of places found in the problem.

Example: **4.53**   2 places
      x 2.2   1 place
       906
      906
    9.966   3 places

▶ To divide a decimal by a decimal, move the decimal point of the divisor to the right to get a whole number.

▶ Then, move the decimal point of the dividend the same number of places.

▶ Divide as usual.

▶ Place a decimal point in the quotient directly above the decimal point in the dividend.

Example:
$$14.2 \overline{)458.66}$$
quotient **32.3**
    426
    326
    284
     426
     426
       0

See also **percent.**

declarative sentence   *See* **sentence.**

degree [°]   A unit of measurement for angles or temperature.

See also **angle, Celsius thermometer, Fahrenheit thermometer,** *and* **geometric figures.**

denominator | The number in the bottom of a fraction. The denominator tells how many equal parts there are.

Example: $\dfrac{1}{8}$ The number 8 is the denominator.

See also **fraction** *and* **numerator.**

desert/dessert | A desert is a hot, dry, sandy region where few plants or animals can live.

Examples: The Sahara Desert is the largest desert in the world.
Dessert is usually the last course at lunch or dinner.

Dewey Decimal System | A way of organizing and numbering nonfiction books under 10 subject areas developed by Melvil Dewey.

000–099 .... Generalities
100–199 .... Philosophy and related disciplines
200–299 .... Religion
300–399 .... Social sciences
400–499 .... Language
500–599 .... Sciences
600–699 .... Technology and applied sciences
700–799 .... Fine arts
800–899 .... Literature
900–999 .... History and geography

diagram | A drawing or sketch showing the important parts of an object or how something works.

Examples:

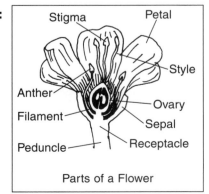

Parts of a Flower

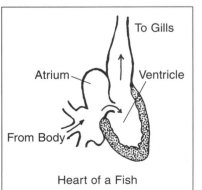

Heart of a Fish

diameter

A straight line through the center of a circle from one point on the circle to the opposite point. The diameter can travel in any direction as long as it passes through the center of the circle.

Examples:

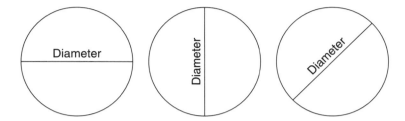

See also **circumference** *and* **pi.**

diamonte

A seven-line stanza having a diamond shape and a definite structure. It begins with a subject (noun 1) and ends with a different subject (noun 2), usually the opposite of the first noun.

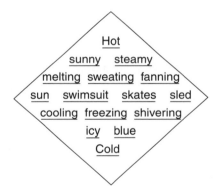

Line 1   one noun—first subject

Line 2   two adjectives describing the noun

Line 3   three participles ending in *-ing* telling about the noun

Line 4   four nouns, two referring to the first subject, and two referring to the last subject

Line 5   three participles ending in *-ing* telling about the last subject

Line 6   two adjectives telling about the last subject

Line 7   one noun—last subject

dictionary A reference book that lists words alphabetically and explains the meaning, pronunciation, and part of speech of each word. Dictionaries may also include synonyms, antonyms, and biographical and geographic listings.

Examples:

A

az - ure (azh´r) *adj.* Of or like the color of a clear sky.
az - u - rite (azh´-rit) *n.* A brilliantly blue, monoclinic material.

B

B, b (be) *n.* The second letter of the English alphabet: from the Greek *beta.*
baa (ba) *n.* The cry of a sheep or goat.

difference The answer to a subtraction problem.

See also **subtraction.**

digestive system The system of the body that digests food, which is used to rebuild and replace cells and provides the body with energy. The major parts include:

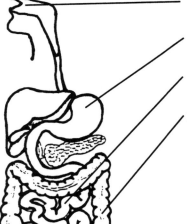

Mouth: Saliva containing enzymes breaks down food.
Stomach: Gastric juices liquefy food into a thick substance.
Small intestine: Most digestion takes place here; bile further liquifies.
Large intestine: Liquids filter out substances body still needs and rids itself of waste.

digit	Any of the numbers 0, 1, 2, 3, 4, 5, 6, 7, 8, 9.
digraph	A pair of letters, either two consonants or two vowels, that together represent one sound.

Consonant Digraphs

br	**gh**	**ph**	**th**
brush	laugh	elephant	thirty
bring	cough	phone	three

ch	**gn**	**sc**	**wh**
chair	sign	school	whip
church	gnaw	scare	wheel

ck	**kn**	**sh**	
check	knee	show	
stick	knot	ship	

Vowel Digraphs

ai	**ea**	**ie**	**oo**	**ue**
train	peach	pies	book	glue
jail	eat	cries	good	blue

au	**ea**	**ie**	**ou**	**ui**
caught	head	stories	out	suit
haunt	bread	thief	couch	fruit

aw	**ee**	**oa**	**ow**	
paw	green	boat	snow	
crawl	feet	groan	bowl	

ay	**ew**	**oo**	**ow**	
play	chew	moon	how	
hay	mew	spoon	cow	

diphthong | Two vowels blended together to represent one speech sound.

Diphthongs

au	**ea**	**ew**	**oo**	**ow**
auto	bread	flew	moon	cow
caught	thread	grew	spoon	town

aw	**ei**	**oi**	**ou**	**oy**
jaw	rein	boil	ouch	boy
awful	sleigh	point	house	enjoy

distributive property | When one factor is a sum, multiplying each addend by the other factor before adding will not change the product.

Example: 4 x (6 + 3)   (4 x 6) + (4 x 3)
4 x 9 = 36   24 + 12 = 36
36   =   36

District of Columbia | A district established from land given by Maryland and Virginia and occupied by the city of Washington, the capital of the United States. It is not a state.

dividend | A number to be divided by another number.

Example: 3)9
The number 9 is the dividend.

In business, a payment of a portion of the profits from a company paid to a stockholder.

divisibility | A whole number that is divided by another number with the remainder of zero.

Divisibility Rules

2   A number is divisible by 2 if the end digit is a 0, 2, 4, 6, or 8.

568   455
divisible   not divisible

3 A number is divisible by 3 if the sum of the digits is divisible by 3.

435   4 + 3 + 5 = 12   527   5 + 2 + 7 = 14
divisible   not divisible

4 A number is divisible by 4 if the last two digits form a number that is divisible by 4.

220   20 − 4 = 5   1,227   27 cannot be divided evenly
divisible   not divisible

5 A number is divisible by 5 if it ends in 0 or 5.

7,730   5,507
divisible   not divisible

6 A number is divisible by 6 if the number is even and divisible by either 2 or 3.

534   4 − 2 = 2   and   5 + 3 + 4 = 12   12 ÷ 3 = 4
divisible

7 There is no divisibility rule for 7.

8 A number is divisible by 8 if the last three digits of the number is divisible by 8.

6,360   6360 − 8 = 795   2,564 can not be divided evenly
divisible   not divisible

9 A number is divisible by 9 if the sum of the digits is divisible by 9.

42,516   4 + 2 + 5 + 1 + 6 = 18
divisible

81,437   8 + 1 + 4 + 3 + 7 = 23
not divisible

10 A number is divisible by 10 if the number ends in 0.

3,000   4,004
divisible   not divisible

division | A way of finding out how many groups of one number can be found in another number.

Example:

15 ÷ 5   or   **5 ⟌ 15**
In the number 15, there are 3 groups of 5.

Because division is the reverse of multiplication, think of a multiplication fact that will equal the dividend.

Example: **3**
5 x 3 = 15   so   **5 ⟌ 15**

LONG DIVISION

To remember the steps used in long division, think of this saying:

Do Monkeys Sleep Bare?
Problem: **3 ⟌ 48**

Do (Divide): How many groups of 3 are in 4?

$$\begin{array}{r} 1 \\ 3\overline{)48} \end{array}$$

Monkeys (Multiply): **1 x 3 = 3**

$$\begin{array}{r} 1 \\ 3\overline{)48} \\ \underline{3} \end{array}$$

Sleep (Subtract): **4 − 3 = 1**

$$\begin{array}{r} 1 \\ 3\overline{)48} \\ \underline{3} \\ 1 \end{array}$$

Bare (Bring down): Bring down the number 8 next.

$$3 \overline{)48}$$

```
     1
3 ) 48
    3
    18
```

Begin again with Do (Divide) and continue until there are no more numbers to bring down. What is left is called the remainder. There are 16 groups of 3 in 48.

```
     16
3 ) 48
    3
    18
    18
     0  remainder
```

See also **casting out nines** *and* **remainder.**

divisor

A number by which another number is to be divided:

Example: $2 \overline{)36}$ The number 2 is the divisor.

E

earth's layers

The earth, the third planet from the sun, is made up of several layers. They are:

Crust: Surface or top layer; consists of a thin layer of rock; thickness measures from three to twenty-two miles; divided into oceanic and continental crust.

Mantle: Layer beneath the crust; consists of hot molten rock; thickness about 1,800 miles.

Mantle
Outer Core
Inner Core
Crust

Core: Consists of two parts: inner core is solid iron and nickel and has high temperatures; outer core is made up of molten rock; is about 1,400 miles thick.

earthquake

A series of vibrations that pass through the crust of the earth and whose force is measured from very slight to destructive.

See **Richter scale** *and* **epicenter.**

ecology

The study of living things in their natural environments.

edit

To review the content and organization of a written work, revise as necessary, and correct errors in grammar, spelling, and punctuation.

See also **proofreading symbols.**

ellipsis [. . .]

Three dots used to show that one or more words were omitted from a sentence or that someone's statement was interrupted.

Examples: An apple a day . . . (omission)
"How much is . . . Hey! What's going on here?" (interruption)

encyclopedia

A book or set of books that contains information on many subjects. The subjects are listed alphabetically.

English/Metric Conversion Table

If you know	To find	Multiply by
inches	millimeters	25.4
inches	centimeters	2.54
feet	centimeters	30.48
yards	meters	0.91
miles	kilometers	1.61
fluid ounces	milliliters	29.57
cups	liters	0.24
pints	liters	0.47
quarts	liters	0.95
gallons	liters	3.79
ounces	grams	28
pounds	kilograms	0.45
short tons	megagrams	0.9
acres	hectares	0.40

epicenter | The area on the earth's surface directly above the site of the earthquake.

epilogue | A short summary following the end of a novel, often dealing with the future of the characters or with future events.

equator | An imaginary circle around the middle of the earth, halfway between the North Pole and the South Pole. The equator is at 0° latitude.

See also **latitude.**

equilateral triangle | *See* **geometric figures.**

equinox | Either of two times in a year when the sun crosses the equator and day and night everywhere are of equal length. These times occur about March 21 and September 22.

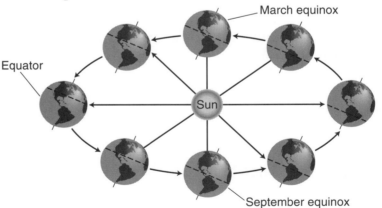

equivalent | Equal; having equal value.

Examples: One nickel is equivalent to 5 cents.
The fraction 2/4 is equivalent to 1/2.

See also **percent.**

essay	A short piece of writing; a composition expressing the author's opinion.
estimate	To figure approximately; to form an opinion or judgment. Not exact.

> **Examples:** Jim estimated that 37 and 22 are about 60.
> I think the battery will cost
> about $90.00 plus tax.

See also **rounding.**

even number	The number 2 or any multiple of 2; any number ending in 0, 2, 4, 6, or 8; any number that can be divided by two.
exclamation point [!]	A punctuation mark used after a word or sentence to give a sharp command or to show surprise, joy, fear, shock, or other strong emotion.

> **Examples:** Help! Watch out! Stop!
> What a wonderful day!
> There's a tornado!

exclamatory sentence	*See* **sentence.**
expanded numeral	A numeral written in expanded notation; a method of showing the value named by each digit in a numeral.

> **Example:** 5,207 = 5,000
> 200
> 00
> 7
> or 5,207 = 5,000 + 200 + 00 + 7

exponent	A numeral written slightly above and to the right of a number to tell how many times that number is to be used as a factor.

> **Example:** In the number 10^3, the numeral 3 is the exponent. It
> shows that 10 is used as a factor, a number to be
> multiplied, 3 times.
> $10^3 = 10 \times 10 \times 10$ or 1,000

fact family

A group of numbers whose result is always the same.

Example: $3 + 4 = 7$ $\qquad$ $4 + 3 = 7$
$7 - 4 = 3$ $\qquad$ $7 - 3 = 4$

fact or opinion

A fact is a true statement; it can be proven.

Example: There are twelve months in a year.

An opinion tells how someone feels or thinks about something.

Example: April is the best month of the year.

factor

A number to be multiplied by another number.

Example:
$$\begin{array}{r} 2 \\ \underline{\times\,4} \end{array} \quad 4 \times 2$$

The numbers 2 and 4 are factors.

factor tree

A diagram used to find the prime factors of a number.

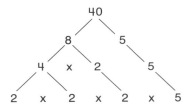

Fahrenheit thermometer	A thermometer that has a temperature scale on which 32° is the freezing point of water and 212° the boiling point of water. The Fahrenheit thermometer was named for Gabriel D. Fahrenheit.

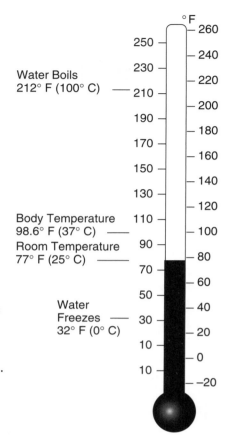

Water Boils
212° F (100° C)

Body Temperature
98.6° F (37° C)

Room Temperature
77° F (25° C)

Water
Freezes
32° F (0° C)

▶ The temperature 80°F is read "eighty degrees Fahrenheit."

To convert Fahrenheit temperature to Celsius, subtract 32 from the Fahrenheit temperature and multiply the remainder by 5/9.

Formula:
Fahrenheit temperature – 32 x 5/9 = Celsius temperature

Example: 86°F – 32 = 54 x 5/9 = 30°C.

farther/further	The word *farther* means a greater distance. It explains space.

Example: Chuck threw the ball *farther* than Charlie.

The word *further* means to a greater extent.

Example: We need to inquire *further* before making a decision.

fault	A break in the earth's crust, with the mass of rock on one side of the break pushed up, down, or sideways.

fiction	Imaginative writings, including stories, plays, and poems.

Examples: *Alice in Wonderland* by Lewis B. Carroll
Moby Dick by Herman Melville

flow chart | A diagram showing the logical steps followed in a sequence of operation.

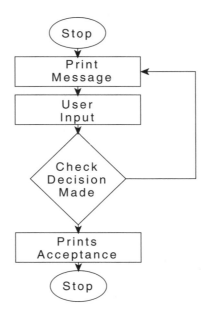

food pyramid | A diagram showing the five basic food groups recommended for a healthy diet.

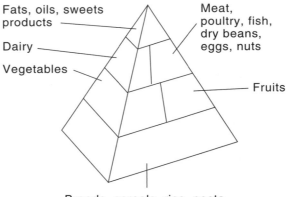

footnote | A note placed at the bottom of a page explaining something mentioned in the text or giving credit to a source.

▶ Announcement of a footnote in the text is indicated by a raised number following the reference.

▶ Number each footnote, beginning with the number one.

▶ Footnotes are usually indented.

▶ Use the term *Ibid.* if a footnote is to be immediately repeated. Write a comma after the word Ibid. and include the new page numbers.

Example: [1]*The Complete Works of Edgar Allan Poe,* ed. J. A. Harrison (New York) Vl (Tales—Vol. V), 241.

[2]*Ibid.,* Vl, 243.

foreign words and phrases

Words and phrases from foreign languages commonly found in printed works.

ad hoc	for this special project (Latin)
bona fide	in good faith (Latin)
bon vivant	party goer (French)
carpe diem	enjoy today (Latin)
caveat emptor	let the buyer beware (Latin)
c'est la vie	that's life (French)
coup de grace	final blow (French)
coup d'etat	overthrow of the government (French)
de facto	in fact (Latin)
déja vu	already seen; happening before (French)
ex libris	from the books (Latin)
ex post facto	after the fact (Latin)
fait accompli	an accomplished fact (French)
faux pas	mistake (French)
ibidem (ibid.)	in the same place; in work just mentioned (Latin)
ipso facto	from the facts (Latin)
laissez-faire	to let do as they choose (French)
nom de plume	pen name (French)
non sequitur	does not follow logically (Latin)
per annum	yearly (Latin)
per capita	by the head (Latin)
personna non grata	unwanted person (Latin)
quid pro quo	an equivalent in return (Latin)
savoir faire	social know-how (French)
sine qua non	something indispensable (Latin)
stet	let it stand; do not correct (Latin)
tempus fugit	time flies (Latin)
tête-a-tête	intimate talk (French)

fossil   The remains of a plant or animal preserved from a past age in sedimentary rock in the earth's crust.

fraction   Two numbers separated by a line. The number above the line is called the *numerator;* the number below the line is called the *denominator.* A fraction tells the number of parts of a whole.

Examples:

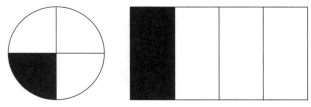

1/4 means 1 part of 4 equal parts (the whole).

2/5 means 2 parts of 5 equal parts (the whole).

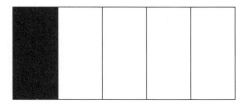

In the illustration, 3/5 of the figures have flags.

▶ Addition of like fractions (same denominators)

Add the numerators together and place the sum above the demoninator. Do not add the denominators.

$$2/8 + 3/8 + 2/8 = 7/8$$
$$3/4 + 3/4 + 1/4 = 7/4 \ \text{(Reduce to lowest terms: 1 3/4)}$$

▶ Addition of unlike fractions (different denominators)

Change the fractions to equivalent fractions by finding the least common denominator (LCD). Add the new numerators and place the sum over the common denominator.

Find the LCD (in this case, 24).

3/8 = 9/24   Divide each demoninator into the LCD.
+ 1/6 = 4/24   Multiply the answer with the numerator.
    13/24   Write the product over the demoninator.

Subtraction of like and unlike fractions is done in the same way, **except the numerators are subtracted instead of added.**

▶ Addition of mixed numbers

Work the fraction part of the problem the same way as for addition of fractions, then add to the whole numbers. Reduce to lowest terms.

4 3/4 = 4 6/8
+ 2 3/8 = 2 3/8
6 9/8 = 7 1/8

▶ Subtraction of mixed numbers

To subtract mixed numbers, the top number (minuend) must always be larger.

See also **denominator, equivalent,** *and* **numerator.**

fraction number line

A number line that shows fractions in order, from the smallest to the greatest.

fraction to decimal

Change a common fraction to a decimal by dividing the numerator by the demoninator, and write the quotient (answer) in decimal form.

Example:
    fraction 7/8 = .875 decimal

Common Fraction/Decimal Equivalents

1/2	50/100	0.50
1/3	333/1000	0.333
1/4	25/100	0.25
1/5	20/100	0.20
1/8	125/1000	0.125
3/8	375/1000	0.375
7/8	875/1000	0.875
2/3	666/1000	0.666
3/4	75/100	0.75

See **decimal.**

free verse

A style of poetry in which there is no rhyme or repeated pattern.

The Lake Was Covered All Over

The lake was covered all over
With bright silverwaves
That were each
The twinkling of an eye.

—Dorothy Wordsworth

friendly letter

See **letter writing.**

galaxy

A large grouping of billions of stars, gas, and dust found in the universe.

geographic terms | Terms used in the study of geography.

Common Geographic Terms

Archipelago: A sea with a large group of islands.

Bay: Part of the sea that extends into the land.

Butte: A hill that rises sharply and has a flat top.

Canyon: A narrow valley with high steep walls; a gorge.

Cape: A point of land that juts out into a body of water.

Channel: A deep part of a river or harbor.

Delta: An area of land shaped like a triangle in which sand and dirt collect at the mouth of a river.

Desert: A dry area with little vegetation.

Dune: A ridge or hill of sand created by the wind.

Fjord: A long, narrow inlet of the sea between high cliffs.

Glacier: A large mass of ice that moves slowly down a mountain. *See also* **glacier.**

Gulf: A large part of an ocean or sea partly surrounded by land.

Horizon: The line where the land and sky appear to meet.

Island: Land, smaller than a continent, entirely surrounded by water.

Isthmus: A narrow strip of land that runs between two bodies of water and joins two bodies of land.

Lake: A large body of salt or fresh water surrounded by land.

Levee: A bank built along a river to keep it from flooding.

Mesa: A hill with one or more steep sides and a flat top, common in very dry areas.

Mountain: A very high elevation in the earth's surface, usually with steep sides.

Oasis: A fertile area with water located in a desert.

Peninsula: A piece of land that projects from a larger land mass into the water.

Plain: A flat stretch of land.

Plateau: Level land usually higher than land around it.

Precipice: A very steep or overhanging mass of rock; a cliff.

Ravine: A deep, narrow gorge, usually made by running water.

Strait: A narrow channel connecting two larger bodies of water.

Tableland: A high plain; a plateau; a mesa.

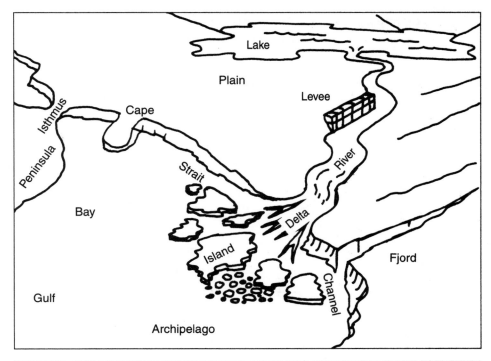

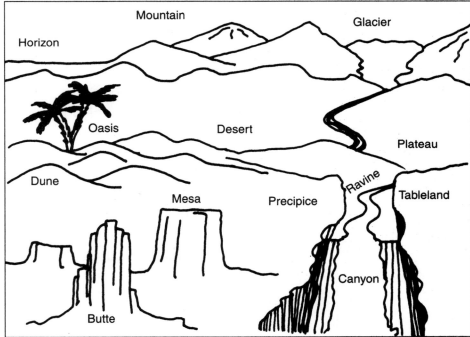

geography	The study of the earth's surface, continents, climate, peoples, governments, industries, and products.
geometric figures	Figures formed from straight lines are curved lines.

Common Geometric Figures

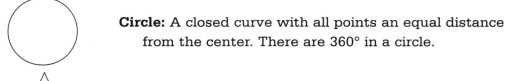

Circle: A closed curve with all points an equal distance from the center. There are 360° in a circle.

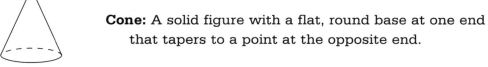

Cone: A solid figure with a flat, round base at one end that tapers to a point at the opposite end.

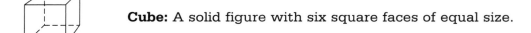

Cube: A solid figure with six square faces of equal size.

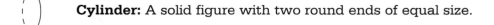

Cylinder: A solid figure with two round ends of equal size.

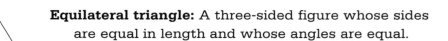

Equilateral triangle: A three-sided figure whose sides are equal in length and whose angles are equal.

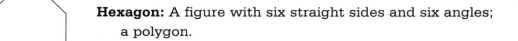

Hexagon: A figure with six straight sides and six angles; a polygon.

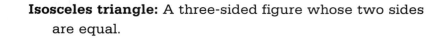

Isosceles triangle: A three-sided figure whose two sides are equal.

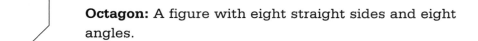

Octagon: A figure with eight straight sides and eight angles.

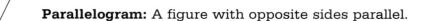

Parallelogram: A figure with opposite sides parallel.

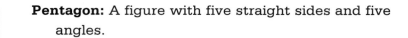

Pentagon: A figure with five straight sides and five angles.

Polygon: A closed figure with line segments as sides. Hexagons, octagons, and pentagons are polygons.

Prism: A solid figure with two equal bases. A prism is named for the shape of its bases.

Quadrilateral: A figure with four straight sides and four angles. A parallelogram is a quadrilateral.

Rectangle: A four-sided figure with four right angles.

Rectangular prism: A solid figure with two parallel rectangular bases and four faces that are parallelograms.

Rhombus: A parallelogram that has all sides equal.

Scalene triangle: A three-sided figure in which no sides are equal.

Square: A rectangle that has all sides equal and four right angles. A square is also a rhombus.

Trapezoid: A figure that has only two sides parallel.

Triangle: A polygon with three straight sides.

Triangular prism: A solid figure with two triangular bases and three rectangular faces.

glacier | A large mass of slow-moving ice located between high mountains and valleys. Glaciers are formed when the amount of snowfall exceeds the amount of snowmelt. They can move at a rate of one inch to several feet per day.

glossary | A list of difficult, special, or unusual words with their meanings, usually placed at the back of a book.

Example:

Archeologist	A scientist who studies archeology.
Basalt	Dark, volcanic rock.
Chisel	A cutting tool for engraving on metal, stone, or wood.
Dead Sea	A salt lake on the Israel-Jordan border.

good/well | The word *good* is used as an adjective meaning "high quality" or "satisfying."

Example: Katie had a good time at the party.

The word *well* is used to show a state of wellness.

Example: Everything is going well at school.

googol | The number 1 followed by 100 zeros.

graph | A drawing that shows the relationship between different kinds of information.

Examples:

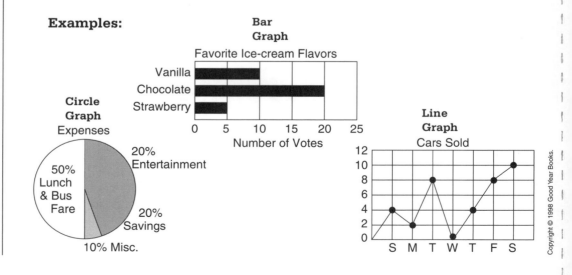

Great Lakes | Five large lakes in the United States. Lake Huron, Lake Ontario, Lake Erie, and Lake Superior lie between the United States and Canada. Lake Michigan lies within the United States.

An easy way to remember the names of the Great Lakes is to think of the word *h o m e s.*

> **H**uron
> **O**ntario
> **M**ichigan
> **E**rie
> **S**uperior

See also **United States of America.**

greater than [>] | A term and symbol used to compare two numbers. The widest part of the symbol faces the larger number.

Examples: 10 > 5   The number 10 is greater than 5.
400 > 200   The number 400 is greater than 200.

greatest common factor (GCF) | *See* **common factor.**

Greek gods and goddesses | The major gods and goddesses in Greek mythology, who are thought to have ruled the universe from Mt. Olympus.

Roman and Greek Gods and Goddesses

Greek Name	Roman Name	Title	Parents	Symbols
Cronus	Saturn	father of the gods		
Zeus	Jupiter	king of the gods	Cronus and Rhea	eagle; shield; thunderbolt; oak tree
Hera	Juno	queen of the gods	Cronus and Rhea	peacock; cow
Poseidon	Neptune	god of the seas	Cronus and Rhea	trident; bull; horse
Hades	Pluto	god of the underworld	Cronus and Rhea	helmet; metals; jewels
Hestia	Vesta	goddess of the hearth	Cronus and Rhea	fire
Ares	Mars	god of war	Zeus and Hera	vulture; dog
Athena	Minerva	goddess of wisdom	Zeus	shield; owl; olive branch
Hermes	Mercury	messenger of the gods	Zeus and Maia	winged sandals; wand; winged helmet
Apollo	Apollo	god of light, truth, music	Zeus and Leto	crow; lyre; dolphin; laurel
Aphrodite	Venus	goddess of love, beauty	Zeus and Dione	dove; swan; sparrow; myrtle
Artemis	Diana	goddess of the hunt, moon, children	Zeus and Leto	stag; moon; cypress
Hephaestus	Vulcan	god of fire	Zeus and Hera	fire; hammer

Greenwich mean time

The basis of the world time zones. The Greenwich meridian is 0° longitude.

grid

A pattern of horizontal and vertical lines spaced to form squares of equal size. Grids are used on maps to locate places and in math to locate numbers.

Los Angeles, Denver, and Miami can be found in the grid below.

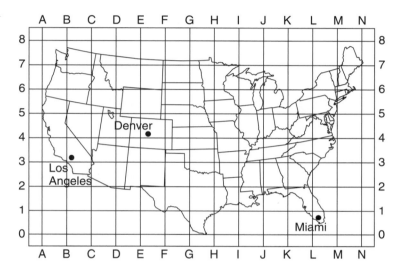

Los Angeles is B, 3
Denver is E, 4
Miami is L, 1

Always locate a point by moving to the right first and then up.

See also **multiplication table.**

gross

A term indicating the total amount before any deductions, such as taxes and insurance.

Gross earnings: A person's salary before taxes or insurance are taken out.

Gross profit: The money earned by a business after it has paid its expenses and before taxes are deducted.

guide words | Words printed in dark lettering at the top of each page of a dictionary or reference book. Guide words show the first and last words printed on the page.

 Help!

To find if a word is listed on the dictionary page shown or comes before or after that page, follow these examples.

To find the word *boom:*

1. Line up the letters of *boot,* the first guide word, and *boom,* the word you are checking. Find the first pair of letters that are different.

> **boot** / **bottom** (guide words)
> boom

2. Does the letter *m* in the word *boom* come before or after *t* in the guide word *boot?*

3. If you answered "before," the word you are comparing will not be found on this page but on a page before it.

Now look for the word *both.*

1. The letter *t* comes after *o* in the guide word, *boot.*

2. Continue to compare *both* in the same way with *bottom,* the second guide word.

> **boot** / **bottom**
> *both*   *both*

3. The letter *h* in *both* comes before the *t* in *bottom,* the second guide word. The word *both* will be found on this page.

Look for the word *box.*

> **boot** / **bottom**
> *box*   *box*

In this case, the letter *x* in *box* comes after the *o* in *boot* and after the *t* in *bottom.* The word *box* will be found on a page after this page.

---

boot / bottom

boot (boot), *n.* **1,** an outer covering for the foot, usually of leather, coming above the ankle: a high shoe; **2,** especially, in the United States, such a covering, either of leather or of rubber, and reaching either the knee or the hip; **3,** a place for baggage in a coach, carriage, or automobile:—*v.t.,* **1,** to put boots on (someone); **2,** to kick.
booth (booth; boo*th*), *n.* **1,** a temporary stall for the sale of goods, for a puppet show, or the like; **2,** an enclosure to ensure privacy.
boot-leg-ger (boot leg ger), *Slang, n.* one who makes or sells something, especially alcoholic liquors, in violation of the law.—*v.t.,*
v.i., and *adj.* boot leg .—*n.* boot leg ging.
boot-y (boo ti), *n.* [*pl.* booties], **1,** food, guns, and the like, taken from the enemy in war; **2,** the plunder of thieves and robbers; **3,** any rich prize or gain.
bor-ax (bor aks), *n.* a white crystalline compound of sodium, boron, and oxygen: used as a cleaning agent, antiseptic, water softener, or the like.
bor-der (bor der), *n.* **1,** the edge of anything, as of a lake; **2,** a boundary or frontier, as of a country; **3,** a narrow strip along or around something; as a handkerchief with a lace *border:*—*v.t.* **1,** to surround or line with a border, as,

haiku An unrhymed poem that has three lines with five syllables in the first line, seven syllables in the second line, and five syllables in the third line. The poem contains only 17 syllables.

Examples: Swift, flying eagle, 1st line, 5 syllables
Soaring high among the clouds 2nd line, 7 syllables
Lost in his own thoughts. 3rd line, 5 syllables

hemisphere | Half of a globe or sphere; the Northern and Southern hemispheres of the earth, as divided by the equator, or the Eastern and Western hemispheres of the earth, as divided by the prime meridian.

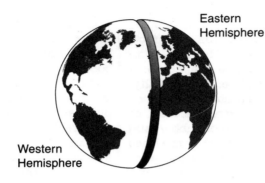

homograph | One of two or more words that are spelled the same but have different meanings, origins, and sometimes different sounds.

Examples: wound   Tom wound the clock.
wound   Bandage the wound.

homonym | One of two or more words that have the same sound and usually the same spelling but have different meanings.

Examples: saw   I saw him yesterday.
saw   Gerry can saw wood.

homophone | One of two or more words that sound alike but have different meanings, origins, and usually different spellings.

Examples: wait   Wait for me!
weight   Watch your weight.

horizontal line | A straight line, usually drawn from left to right, parallel to the plane of the horizon and level ground.

Example:

_____

hydrosphere | The water on the earth's surface and in its atmosphere.

hyperbole | An expression or figure of speech that greatly exaggerates the truth.

Example: I've heard that excuse a million times.

hyphen [-] | A punctuation mark used to join the parts of a compound word or to follow the first part of a word divided at the end of a line.

 Help!

▶ Use a hyphen to join some compound words.

Examples: self-control   fifty-one
one-half   sister-in-law
drive-in   vice-president

▶ Use a hyphen when two or more words are used as an adjective and come before the word they modify.

Example: That was a fast-paced race.

▶ Do not use a hyphen with an adverb ending in -*ly* used with an adjective or a participle.

Example: She will not buy a poorly built car.

▶ Use a hyphen to divide a word at the end of a line.

Example: Jan and I are going to divide that piece of cake.

▶ Use a hyphen when a prefix and a proper noun are to be joined.

Example: un-American   pro-Catholic

hypotenuse | The longest side of a right triangle.

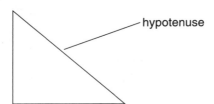

hypotenuse

I/me | When *I* or *me* is used with a noun or another pronoun, be polite: use *I* or *me* last.

Examples: Cissy and *I* love pizza. (with a noun)
You and *I* can share these crayons. (with a pronoun)
The baby laughed at Steve and *me.*
The dog followed her and me.

▶ To decide whether to use *I* or *me* in a sentence, cover the noun or other pronoun and decide if the sentence is correct.

Examples: Barbara and me went to the movies
Barbara and I went to the movies.

Cover up *Barbara* and read the first sentence. "Me went to the movies" is not correct. "I went to the movies" is correct.

ibid. | An abbreviation for the Latin word, *ibidem,* used in footnotes to refer to a footnote just mentioned.

See **footnote.**

idiom | An expression or saying with words that are not meant literally; the words say one thing but mean another.

> **Examples:** "You *put your foot in your mouth*" means you said something you shouldn't have.
> "Sarah is *sitting on top of the world*" means Sarah is feeling extremely happy.

igneous rock | One of three types of rock. It is formed from hot, runny magma (molten rock), which cools and then hardens. Common forms of igneous rock include basalt, granite, and obsidian.

See **sedimentary rock** *and* **metamorphic rock.**

imperative sentence | *See* **sentence.**

improper fraction | A fraction whose numerator (top number) is greater than or equal to the denominator (bottom number).

> **Examples:** 4/3; 7/5; 9/8; 12/12

▶ Change an improper fraction to a mixed number by dividing the numerator by the denominator.

$$\frac{9}{8} = 8\overline{)9}\ \ \begin{array}{c}1\\ \underline{8}\\ 1\end{array} = 1\frac{1}{8}$$

▶ Change a mixed number to an improper fraction by multiplying the whole number by the denominator, and add the numerator to the product.

$$2\frac{3}{4} = (2 \times 4) + 3 = \frac{11}{4}$$

index | An alphabetized list of names and topics discussed in a book. The index is usually found in the back of a book. It tells on what page a topic may be found.

> **Example:** **A**
> Abilene, 175
> Alabama, 17, 46, 89
> Alga, 22
> Arizona, 43, 187
> **B**
> Bill of Rights, 4, 150
> Boa, rosy, 189
> Boone, Daniel, 100
> Boston Tea Party, 199

inference | A conclusion usually based on facts or evidence.

> **Examples:** What inference did you make when the motor lost power? What inference did you make when you saw lipstick on the rim of the cup?

infinity | A space, distance, period of time, or quantity that has no limit or end. The symbol for infinity is ∞.

initial | The first letter of a word or name.

▶ Initials used in people's names are capitalized and followed by a period.

> **Examples:** Thomas Ralph Jones   T. R. Jones
> Julie Collins Morley   J. C. Morley

▶ Initials for other proper nouns are capitalized and often followed by a period.

> **Examples:** B.C.   P.O.   R.S.V.P.
> Exceptions: NASA   PTA   USA

integer

Any whole number. Negative numbers, positive numbers, and zero are integers.

Examples: –319, –42, 0, 1, 3, 257

interest

A charge paid for borrowing money, usually a percentage of the amount borrowed.

▶ **Simple Interest Formula: I = P x R x T**

interest = principal amount borrowed   x rate (percentage)   x time

            $400   x 8%   x one year

       (P)   **(R)**   **(T)**

Interest on $400 would be $32.00 for one year.

Simple interest is based on borrowing money for one year. To calculate the simple interest for more than one year, multiply one year's interest amount by the number of years.

interjection

Words used to express a strong feeling or to attract the reader's attention.

▶ If the interjection is followed by an exclamation mark, the next word begins with a capital letter.

     Example: Hey! That's mine.
                  Hurry! The sale ends Saturday.

▶ If the interjection is part of the sentence and is followed by a comma, the next word does not begin with a capital letter.

     Example: No, you can't come with me, Amy.
                  Oh, why did this happen to me?

International Date Line

The imaginary line that extends north and south at 180° longitude. Areas east of the date line are one day earlier than those to the west.

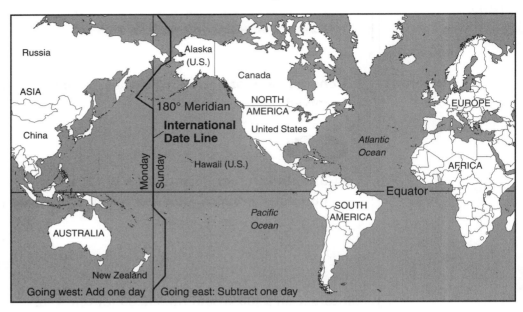

Internet words

Article: A message posted to a newsgroup.

Body: The part of an E-mail that has the most important information or message.

Bookmarks: Pointers used to mark often-used Web pages or menus on the Internet. Bookmarks are kept in lists.

Browser: A program for navigating the World Wide Web and downloading information from it.

Chat: Communicating (talking) online by typing words on the computer.

Cyberspace: Where people and computers meet.

Database: A collection of information related to a specific topic or category.

Default home page: The first page that appears on the screen when you load a browser.

Discussion group: A type of electronic mailing list.

Discussion list: A mailing list that encourages subscribers to exchange ideas and information.

Domain name: The name given to a host computer on the Internet.

Dot: The word used instead of "period" when talking about Internet addresses.

Download: The transferring of data from one computer to another.

E-mail: Messages, documents, and pictures sent and received by computer.

FAQ: Stands for Frequently Asked Questions and used when you need information on a subject. The file name usually ends with .faq.

File transfer protocol (FTP): a part of a software program that allows access to files from other computers or that sends files to other computers-FTP.

Freenet: A bulletin board system designed to give information, usually sponsored by community groups, free of charge.

Gopher: A software program that gives access to online libraries.

Header: Phrase at the start of a message to tell what the message is about.

Host: A computer that is directly linked to the Internet.

Hyperlink: An address connection in hypertext that allows you to link up to other locations.

Internet: A large collection of different networks linked together using modems, telephone lines, and software to enable the user to communicate globally

Key word: Important word that tell you what a document is about.

Log in/log on: To connect to a system.

Log off: To quit and disconnect from a system.

Modem: A device that allows a computer to link up with other computers through the phone lines; a shortened version of modulator-demodulator.

Network: A group of computers linked together to allow data to be exchanged.

Newbie: A new user of the Internet.

Online: The user is connected to another computer system.

Surfing: Using the computer to travel through cyberspace.

World Wide Web: The fastest growing system on the Internet, providing its users access to data all over the world.

interrogative sentence

See **sentence.**

intersecting lines | Two lines that cross (intersect) at one point.

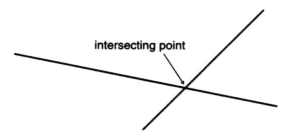

intersecting point

irregular verb | *See* **verb, irregular.**

isosceles triangle | *See* **angle.**

italics | A style of printing where the letters slant to the right, often used to call special attention to certain words or passages.

> **Example:** Mind your *p*'s and *q*'s.
> Do you know the meaning of *e pluribus unum*?
> We're sailing on the *Queen Elizabeth II* to England.

its/it's | The word *its* is an adjective meaning "belonging to it."

> **Examples:** The dog chased *its* tail.

The word *it's* is a contraction meaning "it is" or "it has."

> **Example:** *It's* ten minutes to nine.

key (map)

A list of symbols and what they represent; used on a map to show where places can be found. A key is sometimes called a *legend*.

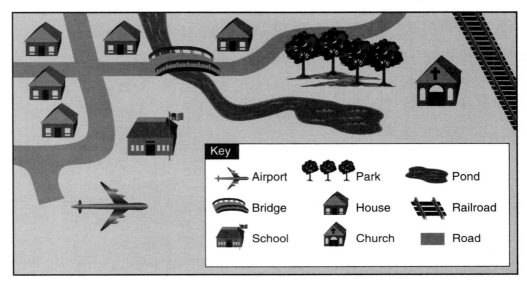

key signature

The group of sharps or flats placed after the clef on a musical staff to identify the key.

See **musical note** *and* **rest values.**

key words

Important words that give meaning to sentences. Key words help you understand the meaning of a sentence more easily.

Example: The long *file of soldiers* moved slowly.

Key words also help you decide what topic to look for in an index to find more information.

Example: How do *Eskimos* live in *Alaska?*

latitude

The distance north or south of the equator measured in degrees. A degree of latitude is about 69 miles. Five of the lines of latitude are named the equator, the Tropic of Cancer, the Tropic of Capricorn, the Arctic Circle, and the Antarctic Circle.

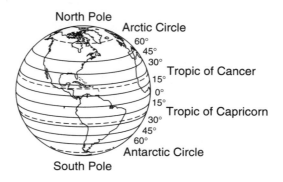

See also **equator.**

lattice multiplication

Multiplication done using a lattice framework.

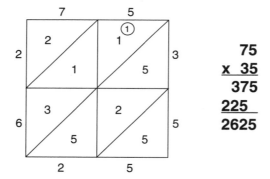

$$\begin{array}{r} 75 \\ \times\ 35 \\ \hline 375 \\ 225 \\ \hline 2625 \end{array}$$

lava

Molten rock that reaches the earth's surface through vents or openings in mountains. Lava reaches temperatures of more than 2,000°F.

lay/lie

The word *lay* means to place or set down.

> **Example:** Please *lay* my glasses on the desk.

The word *lie* means to be in a resting position.

> **Example:** Young children usually *lie* down for an afternoon nap.

leap year

See **calendar.**

learn/teach

The word *learn* is a verb meaning to gain knowledge.

> **Example:** You're never too old to *learn*.

The word *teach* is a verb meaning to help to learn.

> **Example:** Carrie will *teach* me to play the piano.

least common denominator (LCD)

The smallest multiple of the denominators of two or more fractions. When adding or subtracting fractions, the denominators must be the same number. If not, it is necessary to find the least common denominator before completing the problem.

> **Example:** $\dfrac{2}{3} + \dfrac{1}{4}$

The denominators are not the same.

Finding the LCD

1. Compare the denominators in the fractions to see if one of them can be used as the LCD.

2. If not, list the multiples of the two denominators to find the smallest common multiple, which will be the LCD.

$$\frac{2}{3} \quad 3, 6, 9, 12, 15$$

$$+\frac{1}{4} \quad 4, 8, 12, 16, 20$$

The LCD is 12.

3. Using the LCD, write the equivalent fraction for each fraction. Remember to divide the LCD by the denominator and then multiply that number by the numerator.

$$\begin{array}{ll} \dfrac{2}{3} & \overline{}12 \qquad 12 \div 3 \times 2 = \dfrac{8}{12} \\[2mm] +\dfrac{1}{4} & \overline{}12 \qquad 12 \div 4 \times 1 = \dfrac{3}{+12} \\[3mm] & \qquad\qquad\qquad\qquad \dfrac{11}{12} \end{array}$$

▶ Follow the same steps when subtracting fractions.

See also **multiple.**

legend (map)   *See* **key (map).**

less than [<]   A term and symbol used in comparing two numbers. The point of the symbol points to the smaller number.

> **Examples:**   3 < 7   The number 3 is less than 7.
> 84 < 96   The number 84 is less than 96.

let/leave   The word *let* means to allow or give permission.

> **Example:**   My mom will *let* me stay up later on weekends.

The word *leave* means to go away from.

> **Example:**   I usually *leave* my office at 5 o'clock.

letter writing (business)

There are six main parts in a business letter.

Heading: The heading shows the writer's address and the date. Write the heading in the upper right-hand corner of the letter. The first line is the house address. The second line is the city, state, and zip code. The third line is the complete date.

Business address: Begin on the left side of the paper, two lines below the heading. Include the name of the person to whom you are writing, the name of the company or place of business, and the address.

Greeting: This is the way to say "hello." Write the greeting two lines below the business address. The greeting begins with a capital and is followed by a colon. Unless you know the person well, use her or his last name.

Body: This is the news or business part of the letter. Indent the first word in each paragraph.

Closing: Write the closing two lines below the body and to the right, lined up with the heading. Begin the closing with a capital letter and follow with a comma.

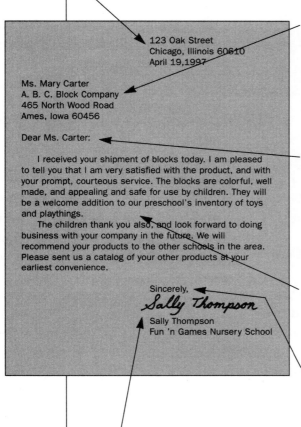

123 Oak Street
Chicago, Illinois 60610
April 19, 1997

Ms. Mary Carter
A. B. C. Block Company
465 North Wood Road
Ames, Iowa 60456

Dear Ms. Carter:

   I received your shipment of blocks today. I am pleased to tell you that I am very satisfied with the product, and with your prompt, courteous service. The blocks are colorful, well made, and appealing and safe for use by children. They will be a welcome addition to our preschool's inventory of toys and playthings.
   The children thank you also, and look forward to doing business with your company in the future. We will recommend your products to the other schools in the area. Please sent us a catalog of your other products at your earliest convenience.

Sincerely,
Sally Thompson
Sally Thompson
Fun 'n Games Nursery School

Signature: Write your full name, unless you know the person well.

Addressing an envelope: The form for addressing an envelope is the same for a business or friendly letter. An address may be typed or handwritten.

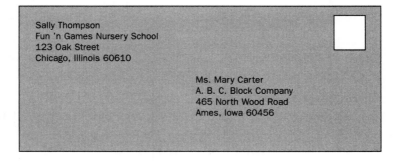

Sally Thompson
Fun 'n Games Nursery School
123 Oak Street
Chicago, Illinois 60610

Ms. Mary Carter
A. B. C. Block Company
465 North Wood Road
Ames, Iowa 60456

letter writing (friendly)

There are five main parts in a friendly letter.

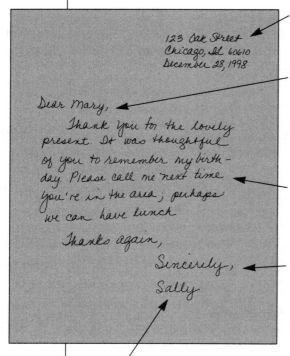

123 Oak Street
Chicago, IL 60610
December 28, 1998

Dear Mary,
   Thank you for the lovely present. It was thoughtful of you to remember my birthday. Please call me next time you're in the area; perhaps we can have lunch.
   Thanks again,
           Sincerely,
           Sally

Heading: Follow the same heading as in a business letter.

Greeting: This is the way you say "hello." Begin on the left side of the paper three lines below the heading and use a comma after your friend's name. Use your friend's first name.

Body: Indent the first word in each paragraph. This is the news part of the letter.

Closing: This is the way you say "good-bye." Write the closing one line below the body and to the right, lined up with the heading. The closing always begins with a capital letter and ends with a comma.

Signature: Write your name below the closing. Use only your first name. If your friend has other friends with the same first name, use your last name, too. Always begin your signature with a capital letter.

Special Forms of Address

The President:

The President of the United States
The White House
Washington, DC 20500

Dear President (last name):

The Vice-President:

The Vice-President of the United States
Old Executive Office Building
17th Street and Pennsylvania Avenue
Washington, DC 20501

Dear Vice-President (last name):

U.S. Senator: The Honorable (first and last name)
United States Senator
Senate Office Building
Washington, DC 20510

Dear Senator (last name):

U.S. Representative: The Honorable (first and last name)
House of Representatives
Rayburn Building
Washington, DC 20515

Dear Representative (last name):

Governor: The Honorable (first and last name)
Governor of (state name)
State Capitol
Name of capital city, state, zip code

Dear Governor (last name):

Mayor: The Honorable (first and last name)
Mayor of (city name)
City Hall
Name of city, state, zip code

Dear Mayor (last name):

Library of Congress classification system

The Library of Congress is the largest library in the world. It is located in Washington, DC. The Library of Congress uses the following classification system to catalog copyrighted materials. This classification system is also used by major libraries.

A	General works
B	Philosophy, psychology, religion
C–F	History
G	Geography, anthropology, recreation
H	Social science
J	Political science
K	Law
L	Education

M	Music
N	Fine arts
P	Language and literature
Q	Science
R	Medicine
S	Agriculture
T	Technology
U	Military science
V	Naval science
Z	Bibliography and library science

light year

The distance light travels in space in one year, about 5,880,000,000,000 miles.

limerick

A humorous poem with five lines. The first, second, and last lines rhyme with each other, and lines three and four rhyme.

> A bugler named Dougal MacDougal
> Found ingenious ways to be frugal.
> He learned how to sneeze
> In various keys,
> Thus saving the price of a bugle.

> -Ogden Nash

"A Bugler Named MacDougal" from *Verses from 1929 On* by Ogden Nash. Copyright © 1935 by Ogden Nash, renewed. Reprinted by permission of Little, Brown & Company and Curtis Brown, Ltd.

line segment

Part of a line having two endpoints.

longitude

The distance east or west of the prime meridian at Greenwich, England, measured in degrees. The prime meridian is 0°. The lines of longitude run from the North Pole to the South Pole.

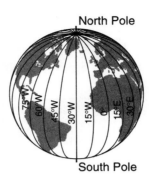

North Pole

75°W 60°W 45°W 30°W 15°W 0° 15°E 30°E

South Pole

See also **meridian.**

magic square

A square chart where the numbers from 1 to 9 in any direction add up to the same sum.

8	1	6
3	5	7
4	9	2

magma

The molten rock (made liquid by heat) under the earth's crust. Magma rises slowly through cracks in the earth's surface. It is called lava once it reaches the surface.

See also **volcano.**

main topic and subtopics

The main topic of an essay is the subject, or main idea. Subtopics tell the details or facts about the main topic.

See also **outline** *and* **paragraph.**

mantle	The layer of the earth between the crust and the core. *See also* **earth's layers.**
map	A drawing of the earth's surface showing details such as cities, towns, mountains, rivers, highways, and other locations of interest.

Thematic

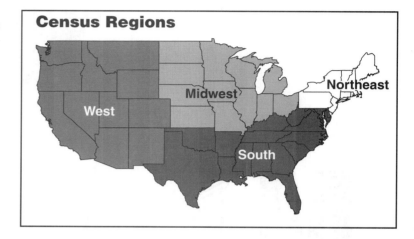

Climate

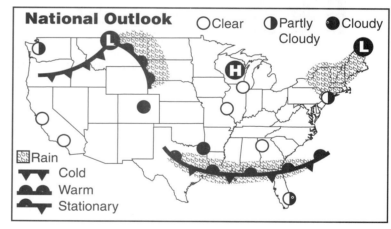

Political

Travel

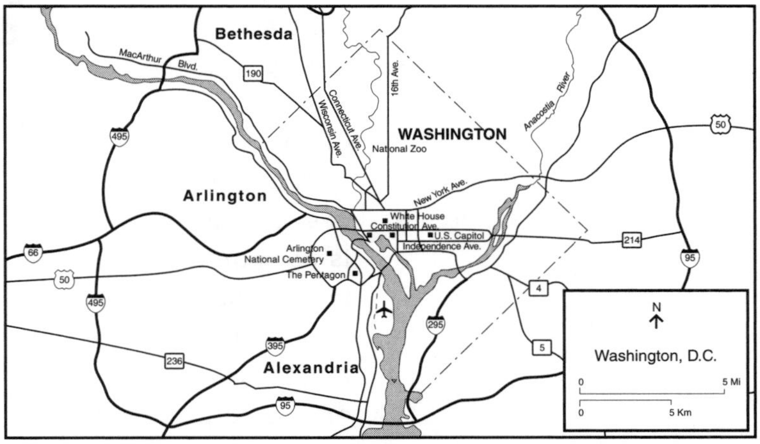

Topographic

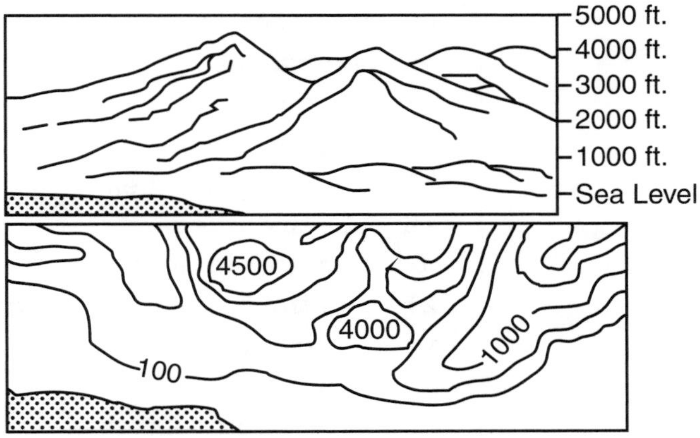

5000 ft.
4000 ft.
3000 ft.
2000 ft.
1000 ft.
Sea Level

4500

4000

1000

100

map scale of miles

A diagram showing the distance from one point on the map to another. May also be shown in words, such as 1 inch = 50 miles.

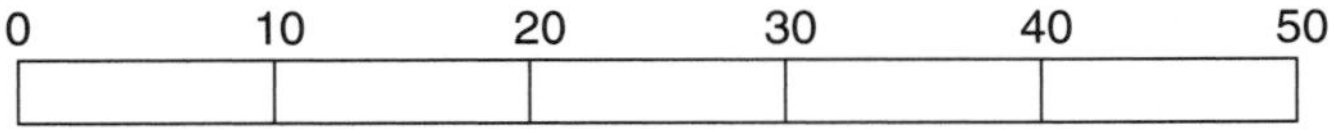

0   10   20   30   40   50

mass

The physical bulk of a solid object.

math symbols	Marks that represent a math process or element.

+   add
−   subtract
×   multiply
÷   divide
⌐   divide
.   decimal point
=   is equal to
≠   is not equal to
<   is less than
>   is more than, is greater than
[ ]   empty set
∅   empty set, null set
∪   union of sets
∩   intersection of sets
≈   equivalent
≉   unequivalent
°C   degree Celsius
°F   degree Fahrenheit
+6   positive integer
-6   negative integer
2^4 2 is the base, 4 is the exponent ($2 \times 2 \times 2 \times 2$)
√   square root
π   pi (3.14159)
⊥   is perpendicular to
∥   is parallel to
%   percent
≤   less than or equal to
≥   greater than or equal to
∠   angle
∟   right angle
∢   arc
≅   is congruent to
@   cost for each
∞   infinity

may/can	*See* **can/may.**

mean	*See* **average.**

measurement   A method of telling size or dimension.

U.S. Customary	Metric

Length and Distance

12 inches (in.) = 1 foot (ft)
3 feet = 1 yard (yd)
36 inches = 1 yard (yd)
1,760 yards = 1 mile (mi)
5,280 feet = 1 mile (mi)

Length and Distance

0.1 meter (m) = 1 decimeter (dm)
0.01 meter = 1 centimeter (cm)
0.001 meter = 1 millimeter (mm)
10 meters = 1 decameter (dkm)
100 meters = 1 hectometer (hm)
1,000 meters = 1 kilometer (km)

Liquid Measure

8 fluid ounces (fl oz) = 1 cup (c.)
16 fluid ounces = 1 pint (pt)
2 cups = 1 pint (pt)
2 pints = 1 quart (qt)
32 fluid ounces = 1 quart (qt)
4 quarts = 1 gallon (gal)

Liquid Measure

1,000 milliliters (mL) = 1 liter (L)
10 liters = 1 decaliter (dk)
100 liters = 1 hectoliter (h)
1,000 liters = 1 kiloliter (k)

Weight

16 ounces (oz) = 1 pound (lb)
2,000 pounds = 1 ton (tn)
100 pounds = 1 hundredweight (cwt)

Weight

10 grams (g) = 1 decagram (dkg)
100 grams = 1 hectogram (hg)
1,000 grams = 1 kilogram (kg)
1,000 milligrams (mg) = 1 gram (g)
1,000 kilograms = 1 metric ton (t)

Dry Measure

2 pints = 1 quart (qt)
8 quarts = 1 peck (pk)
4 pecks = 1 bushel (bu)

See also **centimeter.**

median   The middle number of a series of numbers given in order from least to greatest.

    Example: 7, 11, <u>17</u>, 22, 30
                  The median number is 17.

meridian An imaginary circle around the earth passing through the North Pole and the South Pole. The prime meridian is the meridian that passes through Greenwich, England, and is 0°. All other meridians or lines of longitude are measured east or west of the prime meridian.

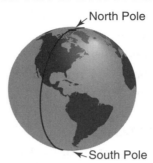

See also **latitude** *and* **longitude.**

metamorphic rock One of three types of rock. It is formed from sedimentary or igneous rock that has been changed by heat or pressure. Common forms of metamorphic rock include marble, slate, and quartzite.

See also **igneous rock** *and* **sedimentary rock.**

metaphor An expression or figure of speech that names or compares one thing to another thing and finds a likeness between them. The words *as*, *like*, or *than* are not used in metaphors.

> **Examples:** Jerry was a *tornado* once he began his work.
> "Their laughter *exploded* in the hall," said Gardner.

See also **simile.**

metric/English conversion table	If you know	To find	Multiply by
	millimeters	inches	0.04
	centimeters	inches	0.4
	meters	feet	3.3
	kilometers	miles	0.6
	milliliters	fluid ounces	0.03
	liters	cups	4.23
	liters	pints	2.12
	liters	gallons	0.26
	grams	ounces	0.035
	kilograms	pounds	2.21
	megagrams	short tons	1.1
	hectares	acres	2.5

Milky Way A galaxy in which our solar system is located and which appears as a broad band of light when viewed through a telescope.

mineral A natural, nonliving, solid substance that has a definite chemical composition. Some common minerals are talc (the softest), salt, clay, gold, and diamond (the hardest).

minuend A number from which another number (the subtrahend) is being subtracted.

Example:
$$9$$
$$-\,5$$
The number 9 is the minuend.

See also **subtraction** *and* **subtrahend.**

mixed number A number made of a whole number and a fraction.

Examples: $6\dfrac{7}{8}$ $14\dfrac{2}{5}$

modifier A word, phrase, or clause that describes or limits the condition of another word.

Examples: We did a *great* job.
The baby *in the high chair* dropped her bottle.

money | Coins and paper made by the government and used to pay for goods and services.

Example: U.S. one dollar = 100 pennies
= 10 dimes
= 20 nickels
= 4 quarters
= 2 half-dollars

Symbols
$ = dollar
¢ = cent

▶ When writing dollars and cents together, it's not necessary to use both symbols.

Examples: $7.25   25¢

months of the year | *See* **calendar.**

multiple | A product of a whole number and any other whole number. A number into which another number may be divided with a zero remainder.

Examples: 3 × 4 = 12
The number 12 is a multiple of 3 and 4.
15 ÷ 5 = 3 (0 remainder)
The number 15 is a multiple of 5 and 3.

Some multiples of 4:

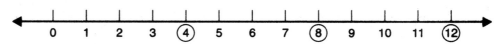

See also **least common denominator (LCD).**

multiplicand | The number to be multiplied by another.

Example: 6   The number 6 is the multiplicand.
               $\times$ 8

multiplication | A short way of adding a number to itself.

Example:

Addition	or	Multiplication
23		23
23		$\times$ 3
+ 23		69
69		

Multiplying Two-Place Numbers

Example: 54
              $\times$ 36

1. Cover the 3 in the tens place with your finger and multiply the remaining numbers in the usual way.

2. The result (324) is the partial product.

      54
   $\times$ 36
    324   partial product

3. Cover the 6 in the ones place with your finger. Note that the 3 is in the tens place. When you multiply with the 3, start your answer (partial product) in the tens place.

      54
   $\times$ 36
    324
  1620   partial product

▶ When multiplying with a number in the tens place, it helps to put a zero in the ones place, so you won't write in the wrong place.

4. Add both partial products to get the answer or final product.

$$
\begin{array}{r}
54 \\
\times\ 36 \\
\hline
324 \\
\underline{1620} \\
1944
\end{array}
$$
   1944   final product

5. Continue these same steps when multiplying 3 place numbers or more. Remember to keep adding zeros so you won't write in the wrong place.

See also **casting out nines,** *and* **lattice multiplication** *and* **multiplication table.**

multiplication table

A chart to help you find the product of two numbers. Use the multiplication table on the next page to find products quickly.

▶ To multiply two numbers, locate one of your numbers in the left column and the other number in the top row.

▶ From the left column, trace across, and from the top row, trace down until your fingers meet on a square.

▶ The number in that square will be your answer, or product.

Example: 4 × 6 =

▶ Find 4 in the left column.

▶ Find 6 in the top row.

▶ Using your left hand, move your finger from the 4 across the row as you move a finger on your right hand down the column from the 6. When your fingers meet on a square, you will find that:

4 × 6 = 24

Multiplication Table

×	1	2	3	4	5	6	7	8	9	10	11	12
1	1	2	3	4	5	6	7	8	9	10	11	12
2	2	4	6	8	10	12	14	16	18	20	22	24
3	3	6	9	12	15	18	21	24	37	30	33	36
4	4	8	12	16	20	24	28	32	36	40	44	48
5	5	10	15	20	25	30	35	40	45	50	55	60
6	6	12	18	24	30	36	42	48	54	60	66	72
7	7	14	21	28	35	42	49	56	63	70	77	84
8	8	16	24	32	40	48	56	64	72	80	88	96
9	9	18	27	36	45	54	63	72	81	90	99	108
10	10	20	30	40	50	60	70	80	90	100	110	120
11	11	22	33	44	55	66	77	88	99	110	121	132
12	12	24	36	48	60	72	84	96	108	120	132	144

multiplier	The number that tells how many times the multiplicand is multiplied.

Example: $\begin{array}{r} 4 \\ \times\, 9 \\ \hline \end{array}$ The number 9 is the multiplier.

musical expressions	Words frequently found in reading music to tell how the music should be played.

a capella	unaccompanied
accelerando	speed up gradually
adagio	slow and leisurely
allegretto	moderately fast
allegro	fast, lively
andante	walking pace
crescendo	gradually getting louder
diminuendo	gradually becoming softer
forte	loudly
fortissimo	very loudly
legato	smooth
lento	very slow
pianissimo	very softly
poco a poco	little by little
rallentando	slow down gradually
ritenuto	slow down immediately
ritardando	slow down gradually
staccato	disconnected, short
vivace	lively

musical note and rest values	The value given to notes and rests to tell the duration of time each note or rest receives.

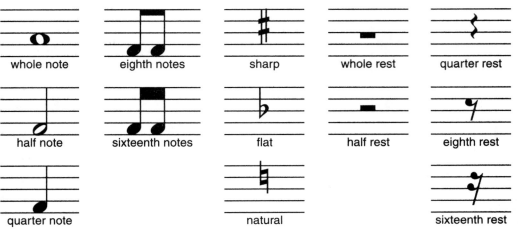

whole note   eighth notes   sharp   whole rest   quarter rest

half note   sixteenth notes   flat   half rest   eighth rest

quarter note   natural   sixteenth rest

▶ A quarter note usually gets one beat.

▶ Sharps ♯ raise notes one-half tone.

▶ Flats ♭ lower notes one-half tone.

▶ A dot ♩. after a note increases the value of the note $\frac{1}{2}$ count.

N

n-gon

A term used to designate a polygon of more than ten sides.

nanosecond

A measurement of one-billionth of a second. Large computers are able to do computations in nanoseconds.

negative number

A number that is less than zero, written with a minus sign before the numeral.

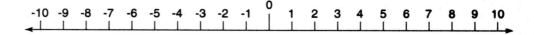

Example: Ten degrees below zero is written -10°.

net profit

The money earned by a business after all its expenses have been paid.

nonfiction

A written piece about real people and events.

Examples: *A Study of History* by Arnold Toynbee
The Sea Around Us by Rachel Carson

Northwest Territory

The region north of the Ohio River and east of the upper Mississippi River, organized by Congress in 1787. It includes the states of Ohio, Michigan, Indiana, Illinois, and Wisconsin.

note/piano key relationship

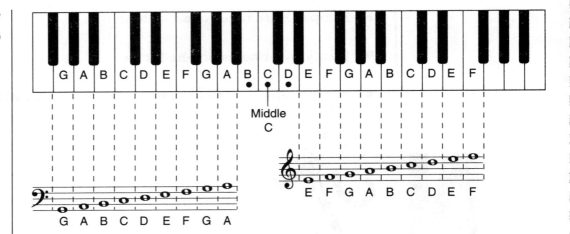

Middle C

E F G A B C D E F

G A B C D E F G A

noun

A word that names a person, place, or thing.

Some Common Nouns

Person	Place	Thing
teacher	school	book
boy	home	jet
astronaut	farm	fork
lady	theater	dictionary

Proper Nouns

A proper noun names a special person, place, or thing. Always begin a proper noun with a capital letter.

Person	Place	Thing
Mrs. Palmer	Chicago	Declaration of Independence
Mayor Jones	Brookfield Zoo	Nobel Prize
Coach Miller	Lincoln Memorial	Medal of Honor

Possessive Nouns

To make nouns possessive, *see* **apostrophe.**

number line | A line showing numbers in order and at even intervals from the smallest at the left to the greatest at the right.

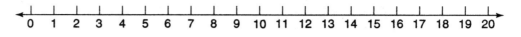

number pair | Two numbers that are used to give the location of a point on a graph.

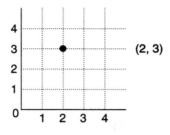

(2, 3)

number prefixes

uni-	one	unison
bi-	two	bicycle
tri-	three	triangle
quadri-	four	quadrilateral
quin-	five	quintuplet
sexti-	six	sextet
septi-	seven	septennial
octo-	eight	octosyllable
nona-	nine	nonagon
deca-	ten	decagon
hecto-	1 hundred	hectoliter
kilo-	1 thousand	kilowatt
mega-	1 million	megaton
giga-	1 billion	gigabit
micro-	1 millionth	micrometer
milli-	1 thousandth	milliliter
centi-	1 hundredth	centimeter
deci-	1 tenth	decigram

number sentence | A number problem written horizontally.

Examples: $5 + 7 = 12$ $(35 - 2) + 7 = 40$

numeral | A symbol written to represent a number.

Examples: 7, 143, 25

numerator | The number written above the line in a fraction. The numerator tells how many equal parts of a whole are named.

Examples: $\frac{2}{3}$ The number 2 is the numerator.

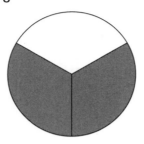

Two parts of three are shaded.

$\frac{2}{3}$ of the whole is shaded.

See also **denominator** *and* **fraction.**

O

oblong | A rectangular or elliptical shape, longer than wide.

Examples:

obtuse angle | *See* **angle.**

ocean   A large body of salt water. There are four great oceans covering about 72 percent of the earth's surface.

Great Oceans	Approximate Area
Pacific	63,800,000 square miles
Atlantic	31,800,000 square miles
Indian	28,400,000 square miles
Arctic	5,400,000 square miles

See also **map of continents** *and* **world map.**

octagon   *See* **geometric figures.**

octave   A musical interval of eight tones having the same sound but at a higher or lower pitch.

odd number   A whole number that cannot be divided evenly by two. 1, 3, 5, 7, 9, or any number ending with these numbers is an odd number. 681 is an odd number.

onomatopoeia   A word that sounds like what it stands for.

Examples: hiss; buzz; pow; bang

opinion   *See* **fact** *or* **opinion.**

ordered pair   A pair of numbers or letters that describe the location of a point on a graph or grid.

The ordered pair is (2,C).

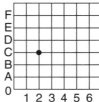

▶ A good way to remember which direction to move first is to "walk over to the mountain, and then climb up the mountain."

▶ Ordered pairs are always written within parentheses.

ordinal number

A number stating a position or place. Ordinal numbers can be written in two ways.

Examples:
1st	first
2nd	second
3rd	third
4th	fourth
5th	fifth
6th	sixth
7th	seventh
8th	eighth
9th	ninth
10th	tenth

See also **cardinal number.**

outline

A plan of organization that shows the *ideas* of a written work, talk, or project. An outline usually answers the questions *what, when, where,* and *which one.*

Form	**Sample Outline**
Title	Vacations
I. Main Topic	I. Summer
A. Subtopic	A. Camping
B. Subtopic	B. Fishing
C. Subtopic	C. Sightseeing
II. Main Topic	II. Winter
A. Subtopic	A. Skiing
B. Subtopic	B. Tobogganing
C. Subtopic	C. Sightseeing

 Help!

▶ The first word in each main topic and each subtopic begins with a capital letter.

▶ Each subtopic is indented under the main topic.

▶ Use Roman numerals for the main topics and capital letters for the subtopics.

Using an outline in writing an essay

1. Begin a new paragraph for each main topic and subtopic.

2. Each paragraph must have a topic sentence that tells what that paragraph is about. The topic sentence is usually the first sentence in the paragraph.

See also **main topic** *and* **subtopics.**

oxidation   The process in which oxygen combines with another substance. When oxidation occurs, a different substance results.

oxymoron   A statement in which two words contradict each other but are used for effect.

Examples: jumbo shrimp   deafening silence

ozone layer   A layer of ozone (form of oxygen) in the upper atmosphere that protects people and plants from the sun's harmful ultraviolet rays.

palindrome   A word or number that is spelled or read the same forward or backward.

	Examples:	dad	level	707
		noon	peep	4,664
		gag	madam	1,221

Pangaea   The name given by scientists to the supercontinent that was thought to exist before continental drift, the movement of plates, caused the land to move and form separate continents.

parable | A simple story told to illustrate a moral.

paragraph | A group of sentences, usually three to five sentences about one subject or idea. This thought or idea is called the *main idea* of the *paragraph*. The main idea is usually stated in the first sentence, which is called a *topic sentence.* The first word of a paragraph is usually indented.

 Help!

▶ paragraphs include:
One main idea
One topic sentence
Three to five detail sentences

Example:

   When you adopt a dog or a cat, you will be responsible for taking good care of your pet. You must provide good food, a balanced diet, plenty of fresh water to drink, and a clean and quiet place for sleeping. Your pet will need to visit a doctor to get booster shots to prevent illness. In addition, you must give your pet a nice area for exercise and play, and most important, lots of love.

▶ The topic sentence is the first sentence.

▶ Types of paragraphs

Descriptive: A paragraph written with many details to create strong mental pictures. Words that help the reader imagine how something looks, feels, sounds, smells, or tastes are used in descriptive paragraphs.

Narrative: A paragraph that tells a story. The writing can be about realistic or imaginary events and characters. It follows a logical sequence of events, creating a problem and ending with a solution. Good narratives keep readers involved with interesting details.

Persuasive: A paragraph in which the writer states facts about a topic to sway or convince the reader to the writer's way of thinking.

Expository: A paragraph that gives information about a topic. It can offer facts, explanations, and directions.

parallel lines

Two or more straight lines that are an equal distance apart at all points.

Example: _____

_____

parentheses [( )]

Language

Punctuation marks used to enclose a word, phrase, clause, or sentence that is included to give further explanation or comment.

Examples: I like to go to the theater (the one next to the mall).
(Did you forget the tickets?)

► If the parentheses occur within a sentence, the punctuation mark goes outside the parentheses.

► If the parentheses contain a complete sentence that stands alone, the punctuation mark goes inside the parentheses.

Math

► Numbers operations written inside of parentheses are to be worked first. This is called the order of operations.

Example: $(2 \times 5) + 5 = 15$

parenthetical expression

A group of words that is inserted in a sentence to add interest but is not necessary to the meaning of the sentence. Parenthetical expressions are always separated by commas from the rest of the sentence.

Example: Chris, _for example,_ is always on time.
However, Marisa is always late.

Common Parenthetical Expressions

however	furthermore	in addition
as a result	meanwhile	consequently
for example	in fact	on the other hand

parts of speech	In grammar, the names of words that function in different ways: nouns, pronouns, verbs, adjectives, adverbs, prepositions, conjunctions, and interjections.

See also **adjective, adverb, conjunction, noun, preposition, pronoun, verb,** *and* **verb, irregular.**

past tense	*See* **verb, irregular.**

pentagon	*See* **geometric figures.**

percent	A hundredth part. Percent tells how many out of 100 are being talked about. The symbol for percent is %.

> **Example:** 80% means 80 of 100.

Percent to Fraction

To change a percent to a common fraction or mixed number, drop the percent sign and write the percent number as a fraction with 100 as the denominator. Reduce to lowest terms.

$$\text{Examples:} \quad 25\% = \frac{25}{100} = \frac{1}{4}$$

$$155\% = \frac{155}{100} = 1\frac{55}{100} = 1\frac{11}{20}$$

Percent to Decimal

To change a percent to a decimal, drop the % sign and multiply by .01. Don't forget to move the decimal point 2 places to the *left*.

$$\text{Examples:} \quad 25\% = 25 \times .01 = .25$$
$$7.3\% = 7.3 \times .01 = .073$$

Decimal to Percent

To change a decimal to a percent, multiply by 100 and add the % sign. The decimal point is moved 2 places to the *right*.

Examples: 0.52 × 100 = 52 or 52%
0.06 × 100 = 6 or 6%
2.5 × 100 = 250 or 250%

Fraction to Percent

To change a fraction to a percent, divide the numerator by the denominator, multiply the quotient by 100, and add the percent sign.

Example: Change 1/4 to a percent.

$$
\begin{array}{r}
.25 \\
4\overline{)1.00} \\
\underline{8} \\
20 \\
\underline{20} \\
00
\end{array}
$$

0.25 × 100 = 25, or 25%

Common Percent-Fraction-Decimal Equivalents

Percent	Fraction	Decimal
12 1/2%	1/8	0.125
25%	1/4	0.25
33 1/3%	1/3	0.333
50%	1/2	0.50
62 1/2%	5/8	0.625
66 2/3%	2/3	0.666
75%	3/4	0.75
87 1/2%	7/8	0.875

See also **decimal, equivalent,** *and* **fraction.**

perimeter | The distance around the sides of a figure such as a square or rectangle. To find the perimeter, measure the lengths of the sides and add.

Example:

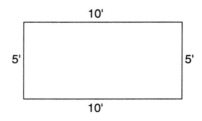

$$P = 10' + 5' + 10' + 5' \quad P = 30'$$

period [.] | A punctuation mark used to mark the end of a sentence or to show an abbreviation.

Examples: Lisa bought a new dress.
Dr. and Mrs. Wilson

See also **abbreviation.**

Periodic Table of the Elements

Key

Atomic Number

| 1 |
| H |
| Hydrogen |

Elemental Symbol
Element Name

1 H Hydrogen																		2 He Helium
3 Li Lithium	4 Be Beryllium											5 B Boron	6 C Carbon	7 N Nitrogen	8 O Oxygen	9 F Fluorine	10 Ne Neon	
11 Na Sodium	12 Mg Magnesium											13 Al Aluminum	14 Si Silicon	15 P Phosphorus	16 S Sulfur	17 Cl Chlorine	18 Ar Argon	
19 K Potassium	20 Ca Calcium	21 Sc Scandium	22 Ti Titanium	23 V Vanadium	24 Cr Chromium	25 Mn Manganese	26 Fe Iron	27 Co Cobalt	28 Ni Nickel	29 Cu Copper	30 Zn Zinc	31 Ga Gallium	32 Ge Germanium	33 As Arsenic	34 Se Selenium	35 Br Bromine	36 Kr Krypton	
37 Rb Rubidium	38 Sr Strontium	39 Y Yttrium	40 Zr Zirconium	41 Nb Niobium	42 Mo Molybdenum	43 Tc Technetium	44 Ru Ruthenium	45 Rh Rhodium	46 Pd Palladium	47 Ag Silver	48 Cd Cadmium	49 In Indium	50 Sn Tin	51 Sb Antimony	52 Te Tellurium	53 I Iodine	54 Xe Xenon	
55 Cs Cesium	56 Ba Barium	57 to 71 * Lanthanides	72 Hf Hafnium	73 Ta Tantalum	74 W Tungsten	75 Re Rhenium	76 Os Osmium	77 Ir Iridium	78 Pt Platinum	79 Au Gold	80 Hg Mercury	81 Tl Thallium	82 Pb Lead	83 Bi Bismuth	84 Po Polonium	85 At Astatine	86 Rn Radon	
87 Fr Francium	88 Ra Radium	89 to 103 ** Actinides	104 Rf Rutherfordium	105 Ha Hahnium	106 Sg Seaborgium	107 Ns Nielsbohrium	108 Hs Hassium	109 Mt Meitnerium										

* LATHANIDE SERIES

57 La Lanthanum	58 Ce Cerium	59 Pr Praseodymium	60 Nd Neodymium	61 Pm Promethium	62 Sm Samarium	63 Eu Europium	64 Gd Gadolinium	65 Tb Terbium	66 Dy Dysprosium	67 Ho Holmium	68 Er Erbium	69 Tm Thulium	70 Yb Ytterbium	71 Lu Lutetium

** ACTINIDE SERIES

89 Ac Actinium	90 Th Thorium	91 Pa Protactinium	92 U Uranium	93 Np Neptunium	94 Pu Plutonium	95 Am Americium	96 Cm Curium	97 Bk Berkelium	98 Cf Californium	99 Es Einsteinium	100 Fm Fermium	101 Md Mendelevium	102 No Nobelium	103 Lw Lawrencium

* rare earth elements
** synthetic elements

perpendicular lines

Two intersecting lines that form right angles.

See also **angle.**

personification

A figure of speech in which an object takes on a human quality.

Example: The palm trees waved goodby as we left Hawaii.

photosynthesis

The process by which chlorophyll-filled plants, using the sun's energy, take in water and carbon dioxide to produce oxygen and carbohydrates.

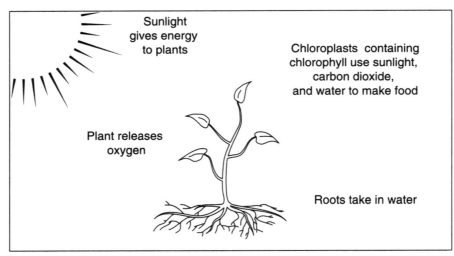

phrase

A group of words that has meaning but is not a complete sentence. A phrase does not contain a subject and a predicate.

Examples: in the park
at the beach

See also **preposition** *and* **prepositional phrase.**

pi [π]

A letter in the Greek alphabet that is used to represent the ratio of a circumference of a circle to its diameter. The value of pi is approximately 3.14159.

See also **circumference.**

pitch

The highness or lowness of a sound. Musical signs that change the pitch are:

Accidental: A sharp, flat, or natural not in the key signature.
Sharp: Indicates a note is to be played 1/2 step higher.
Flat: Indicates a note is to be played 1/2 step lower.
Natural: Cancels a sharp or flat.

place value

The value given to a digit based on its position in a number.

period name	trillion			billion			million			thousand			units		
	hundred trillions	ten trillions	trillions	hundred billions	ten billions	billions	hundred millions	ten millions	millions	hundred thousands	ten thousands	thousands	hundreds	tens	ones
numerals															

▶ A comma separates each new period.

Periods following trillion are, quadrillion, quintillion, sextillion, septillion, octillion, nonillion, and decillion.

planet

A heavenly body in the solar system; a planet moves around the sun. There are nine planets in the solar system:

Mercury	Saturn
Venus	Uranus
Earth	Neptune
Mars	Pluto
Jupiter	

An easy way to remember the planets in order of their distance from the sun:

My Very Easy Method—Just Set Up Nine Planets

Planet Data (approx.)

Planet	Distance from sun	Diameter	Orbital speed	Length of year	Length of day	Surface Temperature	Satellites (moons)	Atmosphere (Gases)
	millions	miles	mi. per sec.	earth days	earth hours	Fahrenheit	moons	gases
Mercury	36	3,083	30	88 days	58 days 15 hrs. 30 min.	-350 to +800°	0	none
Venus	67	7,503	22	225 days	243 days 14 min.	+895°	0	carbon dioxide
Earth	93	7,927	18.5	365.26 days	24 hrs.	-158 to +135°	1	nitrogen, oxygen
Mars	141	4,221	15	687 days	24 hrs. 37 min.	-248 to +77°	2	carbon dioxide
Jupiter	483	88,735	8.1	4,330 11.86 yrs.	9 hrs. 55 min.	-240°	16	hydrogen, helium
Saturn	888	74,975	6	10,760 29.46 yrs.	10 hrs. 39 min.	-290°	21	hydrogen, helium
Uranus	1,785	31,763	4.2	30,685 84.01 yrs.	17 hrs. 14 min.	-350°	15	hydrogen, helium, methane
Neptune	2,795	30,540	3.4	60,190 164.8 yrs.	16 hrs. 7 min.	-360°	8	hydrogen, helium, methane
Pluto	3,666	1,430	3	90,800 248.5 yrs.	6 days	-380°	1	methane

plates | *See* **tectonic plates.**

plot | The incidents and action of a story. The plot consists of the following parts:

Exposition: Sets the scene, introduces characters, gives information necessary to further the plot.

Rising action: The core of the story, usually introducing the problems, goals, or complications that the characters are facing and that lead to the climax.

Climax: The high point or turning point of the story that decides the direction the story will take.

Falling action: The explaining of the problems or complications needed to bring the story to an end.

Resolution: The end of the story.

plural | The form of a word that means more than one.

▶ To form the plural of most nouns, add *s*.

Examples: girl   girl*s*
truck   truck*s*
pin   pin*s*
shoe   shoe*s*
flower   flower*s*
step   step*s*

▶ Add *es* to singular nouns that end in the following letters:
   s   ss   sh   ch   x   z

   Examples: gas   gas*es*
                 mass   mass*es*
                 bush   bush*es*
                 church church*es*
                 fox   fox*es*
                 buzz   buzz*es*

▶ Add *es* to some words that end in o.

   Examples: potato   potato*es*
                 hero   hero*es*

            Some exceptions:
            radio   radio*s*
            piano   piano*s*

▶ When the singular nouns end in a consonant and *y*, change the *y* to *i* and add *es*.

   Examples: story   stor*ies*
                 baby   bab*ies*
                 lady   lad*ies*

▶ For most nouns ending in *f* or *fe*, change the *f* to *v* and add *es*.

   Examples: knife   kni*ves*
                 loaf   loa*ves*
                 thief   thie*ves*
                 half   hal*ves*

▶ Some nouns have the same spelling for singular and plural forms.

   Examples: deer   deer
                 sheep   sheep
                 moose   moose
                 trout   trout

▶ Some nouns form plurals by changing their spelling.

Examples:
man	men
child	children
goose	geese
foot	feet
mouse	mice
woman	women

See also **apostrophe** *and* **verb.**

p.m.
(post meridiem)

Post meridiem; used to show the time from after noon to midnight.

Examples: 3:00 p.m.   8:30 p.m.   11:59 p.m.

possessive nouns

See **apostrophe.**

predicate

Word or words in a sentence that tell something about the subject. The predicate includes a verb and often includes words that modify or complement the verb or a noun.

Examples: Phillip *lost his tennis racket.*
Pat *is talking on the phone.*
Mom *gave me a cookie.*
Her sister *is a doctor.*

prefix | A syllable added to the beginning of a word to change the meaning of the word.

Common Prefixes

Prefix	Meaning	Example
aero-	air	aerospace, aeronautic
anti-	against	anticlimax, antifreeze
auto-	self	automatic, autograph
bi-	two	bicycle, bilingual
bio-	life	biochemist, biography
com-	with, together	compound, commit
con-	with	connect, conform
de-	down, from	deflate, depart
dis-	not	dishonest, disappear
ex-	out	export, exclude
inter-	between	interchange, interlock
mis-	wrong	misspell, misplace
non-	not	nonliving, nonskid
post-	after	postscript, postpone
pre-	before	preschool, prepaid
re-	again, back	reheat, return
sub-	below	submarine, subway
trans-	across	transform, transport
tri-	three	tricycle, triplets
un-	not, opposite of	unhappy, unclean
uni-	one	unicycle, unicorn

preposition

A word that relates a noun or pronoun to some other word in a sentence. A preposition is followed by an object and begins a prepositional phrase.

> **Example:** He put the present *on the table*.

Some Common Prepositions

about	before	during	off	until
above	behind	except	on	up
across	below	for	out	upon
after	beneath	from	over	with
against	beside	in	through	without
along	between	into	throughout	
among	by	like	to	
around	beyond	near	toward	
at	down	of	under	

prepositional phrase

A phrase beginning with a preposition and ending with a noun or pronoun. The phrase modifies a noun, pronoun, verb, or adjective and shows a relationship in time or space.

> **Example:** *In a few minutes*, the man *on the boat* will dive *into the water*.

present tense

See **verb.**

presidential succession order	The sequence of order to govern the United States in the event the President dies or is impeached.

1st	Vice-President
2nd	Speaker of the House
3rd	President pro tempore of the Senate
4th	Secretary of state
5th	Secretary of the treasury
6th	Secretary of defense
7th	Attorney general
8th	Secretary of the interior
9th	Secretary of agriculture
10th	Secretary of commerce
11th	Secretary of labor
12th	Secretary of health and human services
13th	Secretary of housing and urban development
14th	Secretary of transportation
15th	Secretary of energy
16th	Secretary of education
17th	Secretary of veterans affairs

presidents of the United States	*See chart of* **Presidents of the United States.**

Presidents of the United States

Order	Name	Term
1st	George Washington	1789–1797
2nd	John Adams	1797–1801
3rd	Thomas Jefferson	1801–1809
4th	James Madison	1809–1817
5th	James Monroe	1817–1825
6th	John Quincy Adams	1825–1829
7th	Andrew Jackson	1829–1837
8th	Martin Van Buren	1837–1841
9th	William H. Harrison	1841
10th	John Tyler	1841–1845
11th	James K. Polk	1845–1849
12th	Zachary Taylor	1849–1850
13th	Millard Fillmore	1850–1853
14th	Franklin Pierce	1853–1857
15th	James Buchanan	1857–1861
16th	Abraham Lincoln	1861–1865
17th	Andrew Johnson	1865–1869
18th	Ulysses S. Grant	1869–1877

19th	Rutherford B. Hayes	1877–1881
20th	James A. Garfield	1881
21st	Chester A. Arthur	1881–1885
22nd	Grover Cleveland	1885–1889
23rd	Benjamin Harrison	1889–1893
24th	Grover Cleveland	1893–1897
25th	William McKinley	1897–1901
26th	Theodore Roosevelt	1901–1909
27th	William H. Taft	1909–1913
28th	Woodrow Wilson	1913–1921
29th	Warren G. Harding	1921–1923
30th	Calvin Coolidge	1923–1929
31st	Herbert C. Hoover	1929–1933
32nd	Franklin D. Roosevelt	1933–1945
33rd	Harry S Truman	1945–1953
34th	Dwight D. Eisenhower	1953–1961
35th	John F. Kennedy	1961–1963
36th	Lyndon B. Johnson	1963–1969
37th	Richard M. Nixon	1969–1974
38th	Gerald R. Ford	1974–1977
39th	James E. Carter, Jr.	1977–1981
40th	Ronald W. Reagan	1981–1989
41st	George H. W. Bush	1989–1993
42nd	William J. Clinton	1993–2001

Vice-Presidents

Order	Name
1st	John Adams
2nd	Thomas Jefferson
3rd	Aaron Burr, George Clinton
4th	George Clinton, Elbridge Gerry
5th	Daniel D. Tompkins
6th	John C. Calhoun
7th	John C. Calhoun, Martin Van Buren
8th	Richard M. Johnson
9th	John Tyler
10th	None
11th	George M. Dallas
12th	Millard Fillmore
13th	None
14th	William R. King
15th	John C. Breckinridge
16th	Hannibal Hamlin, Andrew Johnson
17th	None
18th	Schuyler Colfax, Henry Wilson
19th	William A. Wheeler
20th	Chester A. Arthur

21st	None
22nd	Thomas A. Hendricks
23rd	Levi P. Morton
24th	Adlai E. Stevenson
25th	Garret A. Hobart, Theodore Roosevelt
26th	Charles W. Fairbanks
27th	James S. Sherman
28th	Thomas R. Marshall
29th	Calvin Coolidge
30th	Charles G. Dawes
31st	Charles Curtis
32nd	John Nance Garner, Henry A. Wallace, Harry S Truman
33rd	Alben W. Barkley
34th	Richard M. Nixon
35th	Lyndon B. Johnson
36th	Hubert H. Humphrey
37th	Spiro T. Agnew, Gerald R. Ford
38th	Nelson A. Rockefeller
39th	Walter F. Mondale
40th	George H. W. Bush
41st	J. Danforth Quayle
42nd	Albert Gore, Jr.

primary colors

In art, the colors red, yellow, and blue. Combinations of these primary colors may be mixed to produce all other colors.

prime meridian

The starting meridian (0) used as a point of reference from which longitude east and west is measured. It passes through Greenwich, England.

Prime Meridian

prime number

A number that has only itself and 1 as factors.

Prime Numbers to 100

2, 3, 5, 7, 11, 13, 17 ,19, 23, 29, 31, 37, 41, 43, 47, 53, 59, 61, 67, 71, 73, 79, 83, 89, 97

probability | A mathematical calculation dealing with the likelihood of an event occurring and expressed in ratios or percentages.

Example: In a flip of a coin, you have a one out of two chance of calling heads or 1:2 (ratio), or 50% (percentage).

product | The result of multiplying one number by another number; the answer to a multiplication problem.

Examples: 6
            × 2
The number 12 is the product.

75 × 22 = 1,650
The number 1,650 is the product.

See also **casting out nines** *and* **multiplication.**

prologue | An introduction or explanation to a story that comes before the story begins.

pronoun A word used in place of a noun. A word that refers to a noun.

	Singular		
	First Person	**Second Person**	**Third Person**
Subjective	I	you	he she it
Objective	me	you	him her it
Possessive	my mine	your yours	his hers its

	Plural		
	First Person	**Second Person**	**Third Person**
Subjective	we	we	they
Objective	us	you	them
Possessive	our ours	your yours	their theirs

Pronouns that refer to the subject of the sentence are called reflexive pronouns.

itself, herself, himself, themselves,
myself, ourselves, yourself, yourselves

See **antecedent.**

pronunciation key A list of symbols that shows how letters in words are pronounced.

Sample Pronunciation Key

ă	fat	ŏ	lot	ŭ	cut	ə	alone
ā	say	ō	go	ûr	fur	ə	item
âr	share	ô	for	ûr	term	ə	pencil
ä	father	ô	taught	ûr	firm	ə	atom
ĕ	let	ô	saw	ûr	word	ə	circus
ē	be	oi	foil	ûr	heard	zh	garage
ĭ	pit	o͝o	book	th	bath	zh	measure
ī	fight	o͞o	boot	th	bathe	zh	vision
îr	pierce	ou	out				

proofreading symbols

Symbols used by an editor or proofreader to let the writer or printer know what changes or corrections are to be made in written or printed material.

Symbol	Meaning	Mark on Paper	Corrected
¶	begin a new paragraph	He ran fast. ¶The race ended	He ran fast. The race ended.
∧	insert a letter or word	The ⌐∧ace	The race
∧	insert a comma	A bright∧cheerful young boy	A bright, cheerful young boy
∧ ⊙	insert a period	She sat down∧	She sat down.
ℓ	take out/delete	Ann went home.	Ann went home.
≡ cap	make a capital	The white house	The White House
/ lc	make a lower case	at the Park	at the park
∨	insert an apostrophe	Tims bat	Tim's bat
⌄ ⌄	quotation marks needed	Get ready.	"Get ready."
◡	close up space	An ani mal	An animal
∿	transpose	The building tall	The tall building

Example:

UNEDITED

i plege allegiaence to the flage the United states of america and to the republic for whitch it stands one nation Under God, indivisile with liberty and gustice for all

EDITED

i plege allegiaence to the flage the United states of america and to the republic for whitch it stands one nation Under God, indivisile with liberty and gustice for all

FINAL

I pledge allegiance to the flag of the United States of America and to the republic for which it stands, one nation under God, indivisible, with liberty and justice for all.

properties of numbers

positive x positive = positive
positive x negative = negative
negative x positive = negative
negative x negative = positive

even + even = even
even + odd = odd
odd + even = odd
odd + odd = even

even x even = even
even x odd = even

odd x even = even
odd x odd = odd

prose   Writing that is not verse or poetry. Forms of prose are articles, editorials, essays, short stories, and novels.

protractor   An instrument used to measure angles and marked by degrees ranging from 0 to 180.

See **angle.**

proverb	A short, wise saying that tells a truth.

Examples: Better safe than sorry.
One good turn deserves another.
A stitch in time saves nine.
He who hesitates is lost.
The only way to have a friend is to be one.

quadrant	One of four areas of a graph formed by the right angles, or a quarter of a circle.

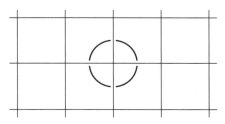

quadrilateral	*See* geometric figures.

quatrain	A four-line poem that follows one of four different rhyming patterns. The patterns include: AABB, ABAB, ABBA, and ABCA.

In a poem using an AABB pattern, the ending words of the first and second lines rhyme with each other. The ending words in the poem's third and fourth lines will also rhyme.

Example:

The Termite

Some primal termite knocked on wood	**A**
And tasted it, and found it good,	**A**
And that is why your Cousin May	**B**
Fell through the parlor floor today.	**B**

— Ogden Nash

"The Termite" from *Verses from 1929 On* by Ogden Nash.

Copyright © 1942 by Ogden Nash. First appeared in *The Saturday Evening Post*.

Reprinted by permission of Little, Brown & Company and Curtis Brown, Ltd.

quotation   The exact words said or written by someone else.

Example: "Ask not what your country can do for you; ask what you can do for your country."

John Fitzgerald Kennedy

quotation marks [" "]   A pair of punctuation marks used to show spoken or written conversation, words, and titles.

▶ Direct quotation: Place quotation marks at the beginning and end of the exact word or words said or written by someone.

Examples: Judy said, "My work is almost finished."
"Why can't I go?" asked Don.

▶ Indirect quotation: No quotation marks are necessary when you are referring to what someone has said but are not using the person's exact words.

Examples: Judy said that her work was almost finished. Don asked why he couldn't go.

▶ Divided quotation: When a quotation is divided, place quotation marks only around exact words spoken.

Examples: "My favorite ice cream flavor," said Tim, "is strawberry."
"I'm hungry," said Jim. "What's for dinner?"

▶ New speaker: Use quotation marks in written conversation and start a new paragraph every time the speaker changes.

Examples: "What's your favorite food?" asked Betsy while they were waiting for the bus.
"Pizza," replied Charlie, with a hungry look in his eye.
"Oh, I like to eat hot dogs," answered Betsy.
"I love all foods," sighed Charlie.

▶ Special words: Use quotation marks with words used to show a special sense.

Examples: The "expert" made three mistakes.
The engine started with a "bang."

▶ Short works: Use quotation marks with titles of short works, such as stories, poems, television programs, reports, short plays, or musical compositions.

Examples: "Sesame Street" is my brother's favorite program.
My report is called "Apes."

▶ Quotation marks within a quotation: Use single quotation marks when you quote within a quotation.

Example: The parent explained to the teacher, "My child told me, 'I don't have to do a report,' but is that true?"

quotient The answer to a division problem.

Examples: 72 ÷ 9 = 8   The number 8 is the quotient.
24 ÷ 6 = 4   The number 4 is the quotient.

See also **casting out nines** *and* **division.**

R

radius

The shortest distance from the center of a circle to any point on the circle.

ratio

The relationship or comparison in size, amount, or number between two things.

> **Example:** 10 children and 1 scout leader.
> The ratio is 10 to 1, or 10:1.

rational number

Any number that can be written as a fraction.

> **Example:** **0.125** can be written in its fractional form, **1/8.**

ray

A part of a line that extends in one direction from one endpoint into infinity.

reciprocal

When the product of two numbers is 1, the numbers are said to be reciprocals of each other; they can be inverted.

> **Example:** $\dfrac{2}{3} \times \dfrac{3}{2} = 1$
>
> 2/3 is the reciprocal of 3/2 because they equal 1.

rectangle

See **geometric figures.**

remainder   The number left when one number cannot be divided evenly by another
number.

Example:

$$\begin{array}{r} 2 \\ 2\overline{)5} \\ 4 \\ \hline 1 \end{array}$$ remainder

See also **casting out nines** *and* **division.**

research paper   A research paper can also be called a term paper. It is a report of 1,000
to 2,000 words telling the writer's ideas and conclusions about a topic
after an extensive study. It includes footnotes and a bibliography.
Research papers include:

1. **Title page**   Title of subject
                     Name of writer
                     Name of course
                     Date

2. **Preface**   An explanation stating any unusual circumstances
                 encountered or special help given during the research.

3. **Outline**

4. **Report**   Includes footnotes.

5. **Bibliography**   A list of all resources used to find the information
                      stated in the report.

See also **bibliography, footnote,** *and* **outline.**

rhombus   *See* **geometric figures.**

Richter scale | A rating system on a scale of 1 to 10 that measures the intensity of an earthquake.

Intensity	Description
2.0–3.4	unnoticeable; instrument detection only
3.5–4.2	slight movement
4.3–4.8	moderate to rather strong
4.9–5.4	strong
5.5–6.1	very strong, causing damage to buildings
6.2–6.9	destructive, causing buildings to move
7.0–7.3	heavy damage to buildings and ground
7.4–8.0	catastrophic
8.0–plus	total devastation

right angle | See **angle.**

Roman numerals | A number system used by the Romans in which seven basic letters were given specific values.

I = 1
V = 5
X = 10
L = 50
C = 100
D = 500
M = 1,000

▶ When a letter is repeated, its value is repeated.

    I = 1
   II = 2 (1 + 1)
    X = 10
   XX = 20 (10 + 10)
    C = 100
 CCC = 300 (100 + 100 + 100)

▶ When a letter *follows* a letter of greater value, its value is *added* to the greater value.

XV = 15 (10 + 5)
LX = 60 (50 + 10)

▶ When a letter of smaller value is *before* a letter of greater value, its value is *subtracted* from the greater value.

IV = 4 (1 from 5)
XL = 40 (10 from 50)
CD = 400 (100 from 500)

root word | *See* **base word.**

rounding | Writing a whole number to the nearest tens, hundreds, thousands, or greater place value. Use rounding when you don't need an exact number.

▶ For numbers ending in 1, 2, 3, or 4, round down to the lower 10, 100, 1,000, etc.

Example: Round 43 to the nearest 10. 43 rounded is 40.

▶ For numbers ending in 5, 6, 7, 8, or 9, round up to the higher 10, 100, 1,000, etc.

Example: Round 572 to the nearest 100. 572 rounded is 600.

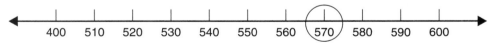

Example: Round 1500 to the nearest 1000. 1500 rounded is 2000.

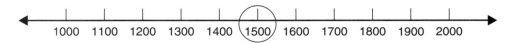

run-on sentence | Two or more complete thoughts that run together without proper ending punctuation.

Example:

Run-on: Mrs. Smith bought Shannon a new winter coat it is red with gold buttons Shannon likes it very much even though it's a little large.

Three complete thoughts have been run together.

Revised: Mrs. Smith bought Shannon a new winter coat. It is red with gold buttons. Shannon likes it very much even though it's a little large.

S

satire | A type of writing in which the writer ridicules or exposes silly human behavior through the use of humor, irony, wit, or sarcasm. Satire is often found in the works of James Thurber.

scale | A series of musical tones that go up or down in pitch.

scalene triangle | A triangle whose sides are all different.

See also **angle.**

schwa [ə] | An unstressed or unaccented vowel sound in a syllable. The schwa ə can represent any vowel.

Examples:
about	ə-bout´
item	i´təm
April	A´ prəl
parrot	par´ət
circus	cir´ cəs

seasons of the year

The four periods of the year: spring, summer, autumn, and winter.

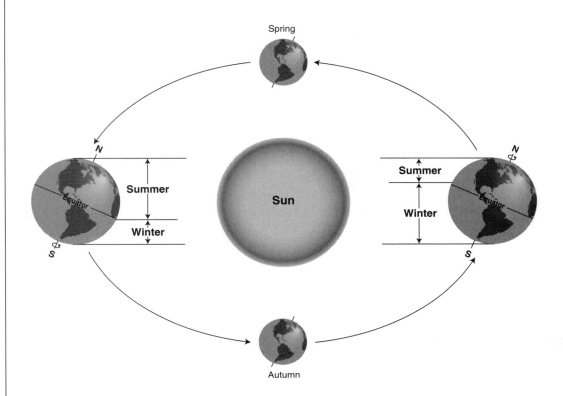

The tilt of the earth revolving around the sun determines the season. When the Northern Hemisphere is closest to the sun, it is summer north of the equator, while the Southern Hemisphere experiences less light and cooler temperatures.

June 21: First day of summer.
December 22: First day of winter.
March 20–21: First day of spring.
September 22–23: First day of autumn.

See also **solstice.**

sector

A section of a circle; a wedge.

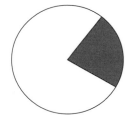

| **sedimentary rock** | One of three types of rock. It is formed from deposited layers of sand, clay, and other materials that settle on the seabed. Common forms of sedimentary rock include limestone, shale, and sandstone. |

See also **igneous rock** *and* **metamorphic rock.**

semicolon [;]   A punctuation mark that shows a separation in a sentence that is not as complete as a period, but more complete than a comma.

▶ Use a semicolon between two separate thoughts in a sentence not connected by *and*, *but*, *or*, *so*, *for*, *yet*, or *nor*.

Example: I have an idea; Jerry has a better idea.

▶ Use a semicolon between a list of items if the items contain commas.

Example: The class officers are Carol Brown, President; Terry Smith, Vice-President; Bob Robb, Secretary; and Roy Toy, Treasurer.

▶ Use a semicolon before a conjunctive adverb (an adverb that connects) when it separates two strong statements.

Example: Climbing this mountain is difficult; however, it is very exciting.

sentence   A group of words that is a complete idea or thought. Sentences have a subject and a predicate.

Kinds of Sentences

▶ Declarative statement: A sentence that tells or states an idea and ends with a period.

Example: We will go to the zoo.

▶ Interrogative question: A sentence that asks something and ends with a question mark.

    Example: What time is the game?

▶ Imperative command or request: A sentence that tells you to do something; the imperative sentence can end with either a period or an exclamation mark.

    Examples: Don't touch the oven!
                Please pass the paper.

▶ Exclamatory exclamation: A sentence that shows excitement or surprise and ends with an exclamation mark.

    Examples: I found five dollars!
                What an exciting show!

sequence The order, when one thing follows another. Sequencing in stories tells what happens first, next, and last.

    Example: **Incorrect Sequence**
                She ate breakfast.
                Paula woke up early.
                She rode her bike to school.

                Correct Sequence
                Paula woke up early.
                She ate breakfast.
                She rode her bike to school.

silent letter A vowel or consonant that is not sounded in a word.

    Examples: knot   The *k* is not sounded.
                gnaw   The *g* is not sounded.
                czar   The *c* is not sounded.
                wrong The *w* is not sounded.
                psychic The *p* is not sounded.

simile

A comparison in which two unlike things are compared; the words *as*, *like*, or *than* are used.

Examples: Bob was as red *as* a lobster.
Jim is *like* a starved animal.
Katie has grown taller *than* a giraffe.

See also **metaphor.**

simple interest

See **interest.**

singular

The form of a word that means one person or thing.

Examples: book   eye
cola   girl
crayon   turkey

Use the word *a*, *an*, or *the* in front of a singular noun.

Examples: a toy
an alligator
the cart

See also **apostrophe, pronoun,** *and* **verb.**

solar system

The area of the universe with the sun in the center and the 9 planets surrounding it, their 54 satellites, asteroids, comets, and dust.

See also **planet.**

solstice | Either of two times of the year when the position of the sun appears to have no northward or southward movement.

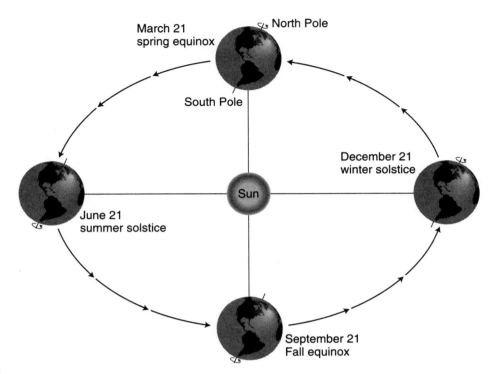

Summer solstice: In the Northern Hemisphere, the solstice occurs around June 21, the longest day of the year. The sun's position is directly over the Tropic of Cancer.

Winter solstice: In the Northern Hemisphere, the solstice occurs around December 21, the shortest day of the year. The sun's position is directly over the Tropic of Capricorn.

March 21 (vernal or spring equinox) and September 22 (autumnal equinox) are times when day and night are of equal length.

sonnet	A fourteen-line rhyming poem that follows a certain pattern made up of an octave (first eight lines) and a sestet (last six lines).

Sonnet

There was an Indian, who had known no change,
    Who strayed content along a sunlit beach
Gathering shells. He heard a sudden strange
    Commingled noise: looked up; and gasped for speech.
For in the bay, where nothing was before,
    Moved on the sea, by magic, huge canoes,
With bellying clothes on poles, and not one oar,
    And fluttering colored signs and clambering crews.

And he, in fear, this naked man alone
    His fallen hands forgetting all their shells,
His lips gone pale, knelt low behind a stone,
    And stared, and saw, and did not understand,
Columbus's doom-burdened caravels
    Slant to the shore, and all their seamen land.

—J. C. Squire

spelling rules	The spelling rules and word study suggestions for all words are:

1. Look at the word. Say the word.
2. Listen to the sounds the letters make.
3. Picture the word in your mind.
4. Memorize the tricky parts of the word.
5. Say the word again, and write it.

However, for every spelling rule in the English language, there is usually at least one exception.

► When adding prefixes to a word, the spelling of the base word stays the same.

Examples: *un*   lucky   *unlucky*
             re   wind   *rewind*

▶ When adding the suffix -*ly* to words ending in *l*, keep the final *l* and add *ly*.

Examples: real *ly*   real*ly*

           beautiful *ly*   beautiful*ly*

▶ When adding the suffix -*ness* to words ending in *n*, keep the final *n* and add *ness*.

Examples: sudden *ness*   sudden*ness*

           mean *ness*   mean*ness*

▶ When adding a suffix beginning with a vowel to a base word ending in silent *e*, drop the silent *e* and add the suffix.

Examples: have *ing*   hav*ing*

           nice *est*   nic*est*

           please *ed*   pleas*ed*

▶ When adding a suffix beginning with a consonant to a base word ending in a silent *e*, keep the final *e*.

Examples: nine *ty*   nine*ty*

           grace *ful*   grace*ful*

           amuse *ment*   amuse*ment*

Exceptions: argue *ment*   argu*ment*

            judge *ment*   judg*ment*

            nine *th*   nin*th*

            true *ly*   tru*ly*

▶ When adding a suffix to a base word that ends in *y* with a consonant before it, change the *y* to *i* and add the suffix.

Examples: happy *ness*   happi*ness*

           greedy *est*   greedi*est*

           hurry *ed*   hurri*ed*

Exceptions: cry *ing*   crying
         bury *ing*   burying
         try *ing*   trying
         copy *ing*   copying

▶ When adding a suffix to a base word that ends in *y* with a vowel before it, keep the *y*.

Examples: relay *ing*   relaying
         play *ing*   playing

Exceptions: pay *ed*   paid
         say *ed*   said
         day *ly*   daily

▶ In words of one syllable with one vowel followed by one consonant, double the final consonant when adding a suffix.

Examples: run *ing*   running
         thin *er*   thinner
         stop *ed*   stopped

▶ When adding a suffix that begins with a vowel to a word of two or more syllables that ends with a consonant, double the final consonant when the word ends with a consonant-vowel-consonant and the accent is on the last syllable.

Examples: be gin *ing*   beginning
         re fer *ing*   referring
         o mit *ing*   omitting

▶ If a word ends in *x*, *z*, *ch*, *sh*, or *ss*, add *es* to form the plural.

Examples: box *es*   boxes
         buzz *es*   buzzes
         church *es* churches
         lash *es*   lashes
         dress *es*   dresses

▶ Memorizing this rhyme will help you remember the *ie* and *ei* rule.

I before *e*
Except after *c*,
Or when sounded as *a*,
As in n*ei*ghbor or w*ei*gh.

Examples: s*ie*ve
rec*ei*ve

Exceptions: cons*ci*ence
so*cie*ty

When the letter *q* is written, it is always followed by the letter *u*.

Examples: *qu* een   *qu* ality

100 Frequently Misspelled Words

accommodate	criticism	Indian	receipt
achieve	daughter	intelligent	receive
afraid	delicious	interrupt	restaurant
against	debt	judgment	rhythm
although	deceive	knowledge	schedule
amateur	discussion	leisure	scissors
answer	disease	library	seize
argument	does	lightning	sergeant
autumn	eighth	mathematics	sincerely
athletic	enough	mischievous	spaghetti
beautiful	equipment	mosquito	strengthen
because	especially	mystery	surprise
believe	exaggerate	mysterious	their
between	familiar	necessary	thief
bought	fatigue	neighbor	thorough
business	foreign	niece	thought
calendar	freight	ninety	through
caught	friend	nuisance	truly
challenge	genius	occasion	twelfth
chief	ghost	parallel	unnecessary
chocolate	government	peculiar	unusual
column	guarantee	physical	vacuum
conscientious	height	piece	vegetable
conscience	heroes	prejudice	weight
convenient	immediate	quiet	yacht

spoonerism	A reversal of beginning sounds in two words. The transposal or switching of the sounds makes the sentence's meaning humorous.

> **Example:** Let me show you to your seat.
> instead said
> Let me sew you to your seat.
> [Named after William A. Spooner]

square root	A number that when multiplied by itself will produce a given number.

> **Example:** 6 x 6 = 36   The square root of 36 is 6.
>
> The symbol for square root is √.

staff	The lines and spaces on which music is written.

See also **clef.**

states	*See* **United States of America.**

stock market	The places where investors, stockholders, and companies buy and sell shares of stock, bonds, and other securities.

Market Words

Bear market: A stock market in which prices of stock go down.

Bond: A certificate of debt issued by a company or government and bought by an investor. The bond issuer will use the investor's money for a fixed amount of time and in return guarantees repayment to the investor of his original investment plus interest.

Bull market: A market in which the prices of stocks rise.

Dividend: A payment to a stockholder from the profits or earnings of the company.

Dow-Jones average: An index designed to measure the movement of the New York Stock Exchange. The index consists of thirty leading industrial stocks on the exchange.

Investor: A person who invests money in stocks and bonds for the purpose of making money on the investment.

Securities: Stock, bonds, and other types of investments.

Share: One piece of stock from a company.

Stock: A share of ownership in a company represented by a piece of paper called a stock certificate.

Stockbroker: A person licensed to buy or sell stocks for investors.

Stock exchange: A place where securities are bought and sold, such as the New York Stock Exchange and the American Stock Exchange.

story elements

The parts of a story that add interest, a logical sequence of events, and a conclusion.

See also **plot.**

straight angle

See **angle.**

stress mark [´]

A mark used with words of more than one syllable to show which syllable is said more strongly.

> **Examples:** accent (ac´ cent)
> repeat (re peat´)

PRIMARY STRESS OR ACCENT MARK (´)

Another name for primary stress mark is primary accent mark. It shows which syllable is said louder than any other syllable.

> **Examples:** vanish (van´ ish)

SECONDARY STRESS OR ACCENT MARK (´)

The secondary stress or accent mark shows which syllable is said with force but not as loudly as the syllable with the greatest stress.

> **Examples:** invitation (in´ vi ta´ tion)
> multiply (mul´ ti ply´)

subject | A word or group of words about which something is said in a sentence.

> **Examples:** *Cindy* is crying.
> *A tall tree* was hit by lightning.
> *The mountains in Alaska* are very high.

The subject includes a noun or pronoun.

Compound subject: A sentence having two or more simple subjects connected by a conjunction.

> **Example:**   *Pete and John* played golf.

See also **sentence.**

subject/verb agreement | The subject of the sentence must agree with the tense of the verb. If the subject is singular, the verb must be singular. If the subject is plural, the verb must be plural.

> **Example:**   The hat is blue.
> singular

> The *hats are* blue.
> plural

subtopic | *See* **main topic and subtopics** *and* **outline.**

subtraction | The process of taking away one number from another number. The remaining amount is called the difference, or remainder.

> **Example:**   8
> − 2
> 6   The number 6 is the difference, or remainder.

WORDS THAT TELL YOU WHEN TO SUBTRACT

How many are left?

Decrease by . . .

How many remain?

Find the difference between . . .

How many fewer . . .

Less

Take away

Minus

PARTS OF A SUBTRACTION PROBLEM

$$
\begin{array}{rl}
56 & \text{minuend} \\
-\,36 & \text{subtrahend} \\
\hline
20 & \text{difference or remainder}
\end{array}
$$

See also **borrowing** *and* **casting out nines.**

subtrahend The number being subtracted from the minuend in a subtraction problem.

Example:
$$
\begin{array}{r}
7 \\
-\,5 \\
\hline
\end{array}
$$
The number 5 is the subtrahend.

Also see **minuend** *and* **subtraction.**

suffix | A syllable added to the end of a word to make a new word.

SOME COMMON SUFFIXES

Suffix	Meaning	Example
-able	can do	capable
-ance	state of being	resistance
-ed	past tense	annoyed
-er	person who does	teacher
-er	state of being more	warmer
-ery	the act of	robbery
-est	state of being most	biggest
-ful	full of	beautiful
-fy	cause to become	liquefy
-ian	one who does	beautician
-ic	like	athletic
-ish	like	prudish
-ish	somewhat like	babyish
-ist	one who does	artist
-ive	tending to	impressive
-less	without	hopeless
-ly	characteristic of	fatherly
-ment	act or state of	amusement
-ness	quality of	darkness
-ology	study of	astrology
-ous	full of	glorious
-ship	condition of	hardship
-sion	act or state of	confusion
-tion	act or state of	election
-y	state of	rainy

sum | The answer to an addition problem.

Example:
$$
\begin{array}{r}
52 \\
+\ 38 \\
\hline
90
\end{array}
$$
The number 90 is the sum.

See also **addition.**

summary

A short statement highlighting the main points of a larger selection. Summaries should:

1. State the main idea in the first sentence.
2. Include only important points in a logical order.
3. Include an ending statement, if necessary.

supplementary angle

A angle that together with another angle adds up to 180 degrees.

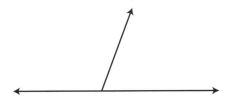

syllable

A part of a word that is pronounced separately. Dividing a word into syllables makes it easier to pronounce.

▶ Every syllable has at least one vowel that you see and hear.

Examples: cat   one vowel = one syllable
per - son   two vowels = two syllables
i - de - *a*   three vowels = three syllables

▶ Sometimes a syllable has more than one vowel. The second vowel is silent.

Examples: treat
be - tween

▶ A one-syllable word cannot be divided.

Examples: dog
mice

▶ Divide compound words between the two words.

    Examples: play-ground
                   fire-fighter

▶ Divide words between a prefix and the base word.

    Examples: *re*-turn
                   mis-place

▶ Divide words between the base word and a suffix.

    Examples: help-*ful*
                   cool-*ness*

▶ If there are two or more consonants between two vowels, divide the word between the first two consonants.

    Examples: la*d-d*er
                   chi*l-d*ren

▶ If the first vowel in a word is pronounced as a short vowel and is followed by one consonant, divide the word after the consonant.

    Examples: rob-in
                   mag-ic

▶ If the first vowel in a word is pronounced as a long vowel and is followed by one consonant, divide the word before the consonant.

    Examples: sp*i*-der
                   l*o*-cate

▶ If a vowel is sounded alone in a word, that vowel forms a syllable by itself.

    Examples: dis-a-gree
                   u-nit

▶ If two vowels are next to each other in a word and each makes a separate sound, divide the word between the two vowels.

Examples: g*i*-ant

i-d*e*-*a*

▶ If a word ends with a consonant followed by the letters *le*, divide the word before the consonant.

Examples: ta-*ble*

bi-cy-*cle*

symmetry

The property of any design or figure that can be divided exactly to mirror itself.

synonym

A word that has the same meaning as another word.

Examples: beautiful   lovely, pretty, attractive

loud   noisy, boisterous, uproarious

See also **antonym** *and* **thesaurus.**

synopsis

A short summary of a book often found on the book jacket or the back cover.

syntax

The way in which words are put together to form phrases and sentences. The usual order is subject (noun or pronoun), verb, and object (the part that receives the action of the verb).

T

table of contents
A listing found in the beginning of a book or magazine that shows the chapter titles, topics, or subjects found in the book and the numbers of the page on which each begins. Sometimes it is simply called *Contents*.

Example:

Table of Contents

Chapter		Page
I.	Indian Tribes of the Plains	1
II.	Homes of the Plains Indians	7
III.	Foods	12
IV.	Religion	18

tangram
A puzzle made up of a square cut into seven pieces. The seven pieces consist of five triangles, a square, and a parallelogram that, when combined, make up different shapes.

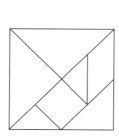
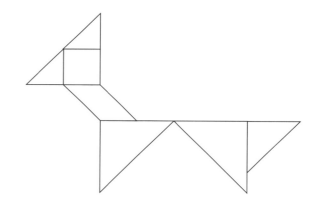

teach
See **learn/teach.**

tectonic plates
Moving plates or slabs that make up the earth's surface. The plates consist of a thin layer of the crust and a thicker layer of the mantle.

term paper
See **research paper.**

tessellation | Tightly fitted, congruent shapes put together on a flat surface to form patterns. A tiled floor is an example of a tessellation.

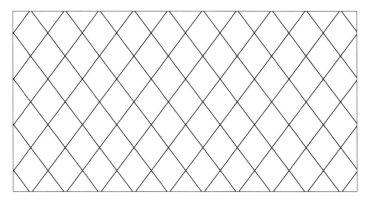

than/then | The word *than* is a conjunction, used to show comparison.

Example: A tree is larger *than* a bush.

The word *then* tells "when" or "in that case."

Examples: He then picked up the telephone. If you want to spend your money, *then* spend it.

their/there/they're | The word *their* is used as an adjective that tells ownership.

Examples: They enjoyed *their* trip to Disneyland.
These are *their* books.

The word *there* is an adverb that means *in that place*.

Examples: Who is *there*?
We will go *there* later.

The word *they're* is a contraction. *They're* means "they are."

Examples: I am glad *they're* here now.
They're driving to Toledo.

thermometer

An instrument that measures temperature; an instrument with a glass bulb and tube marked with a scale and containing mercury or other liquid that rises or falls as the temperature changes.

See also **Celsius thermometer** *and* **Fahrenheit thermometer.**

thesaurus

A book of synonyms or words that have similar meanings. Some thesauruses also include antonyms, or opposites, for each synonym.

> **Example:** **Large:** Big, huge, massive, enormous, immense, grand, gigantic.
> **Antonym:** Small, little, tiny, petite.

tides

The regular rise and fall of the surface level of the oceans, seas, and lakes caused by the pull of the sun's and moon's gravity on earth.

> **Types**
> **Ebb or low tide:** Water at its lowest level at the shore.
> **Flood or high tide:** Water at its highest level at the shore.
> **High spring tide:** Occurs twice a month during the new and full moons.
> **Neap tide:** Occurs when the sun and moon are at 90° angles.

time

The moment when something occurs. The duration of an event, or how long events and happenings take.

The two hands on a clock or watch tell what time it is.

The *hour hand* is the *shorter* hand. It tells the hour.

The *minute hand* is the *longer* hand. It tells how many minutes before or after the hour.

5:40 or
20 minutes before 6

7:25 or
25 minutes after 7

TIME

60 seconds (sec)	1 minute (min)
60 minutes	1 hour (hr)
24 hours	1 day (d)
7 days	1 week (wk)
4 weeks	1 month (mo)
52 weeks	1 year (yr)
12 months	1 year
10 years	1 decade
100 years	1 century (c)
1000 years	1 millennium

Military time uses a 24-hour system of counting hours. The zeros at the beginning of the number are pronounced "oh."

MILITARY TIME

0000 hours	midnight	1200 hours	noon
0100 hours	1 A.M.	1300 hours	1 P.M.
0200 hours	2 A.M.	1400 hours	2 P.M.
0300 hours	3 A.M.	1500 hours	3 P.M.
0400 hours	4 A.M.	1600 hours	4 P.M.
0500 hours	5 A.M.	1700 hours	5 P.M.
0600 hours	6 A.M.	1800 hours	6 P.M.
0700 hours	7 A.M.	1900 hours	7 P.M.
0800 hours	8 A.M.	2000 hours	8 P.M.
0900 hours	9 A.M.	2100 hours	9 P.M.
1000 hours	10 A.M.	2200 hours	10 P.M.
1100 hours	11 A.M.	2300 hours	11 P.M.
1200 hours	12 A.M.	2400 hours	12 midnight

See also **calendar.**

time line	A diagram that gives information about historical happenings, dates, and events at a glance.

Example:

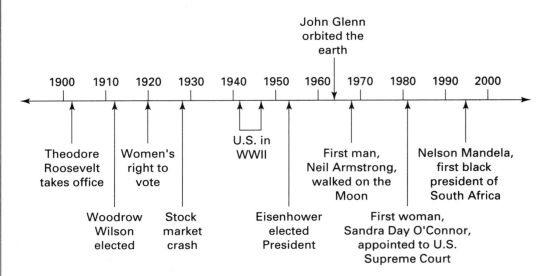

time signature	Two numbers, one on top of the other, placed on a musical staff to indicate the rhythm. The top number tells how many beats or counts there will be in a measure. The bottom number tells what kind of note (quarter, half, or eighth note) will get one beat.

> **Example:** 3/4 time indicates three beats to a measure; each quarter note gets one beat

time zones	There are four time zones in the continental United States: Pacific, Mountain, Central, and Eastern. Alaska and Hawaii are in separate time zones.

See also **United States of America.**

to/too/two

The word *to* shows the way or gives directions.

> **Examples:** Please come *to* my party.
> We read words from left *to* right.

The word *too* means "also" or "more than enough."

> **Examples:** I am tired, *too*.
> I ate *too* much.

The word *two* is a number.

> **Examples:** Tom has *two* pets: a dog and a cat.
> I ate *two* pieces of cake.

topic sentence

The sentence in a paragraph that tells the main idea of the paragraph. The topic sentence is often the first sentence in a paragraph.

See also **main topic and subtopics** *and* **paragraph.**

Tropic of Cancer

An imaginary line 1,600 miles (23°27′) north of the equator; the northern boundary of the tropical zone. In the tropics, where the sun shines down almost straight at noon every day, the weather is very warm.

See also **latitude.**

Tropic of Capricorn

An imaginary line 1,600 miles (23°27′) south of the equator; the southern boundary of the tropical zone. The sun is almost directly overhead at noon every day, and the temperatures are quite high.

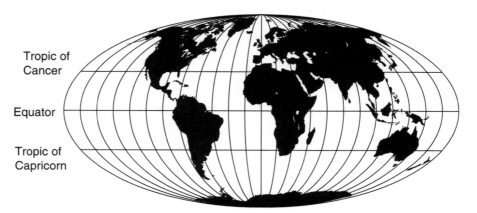

See also **latitude.**

underlining

Underlining is used with titles of books, magazines, newspapers, movies, television programs, and plays when the copy is handwritten or typed.

> **Example:** <u>Babe</u> is one of my favorite movies.
> I read the article in <u>The Chicago Tribune.</u>

When the copy is printed, use *italics* instead of <u>underlining.</u>

unit

One of something; another name for one.

    10 units = 1 ten

United States court system

The third branch of the government.

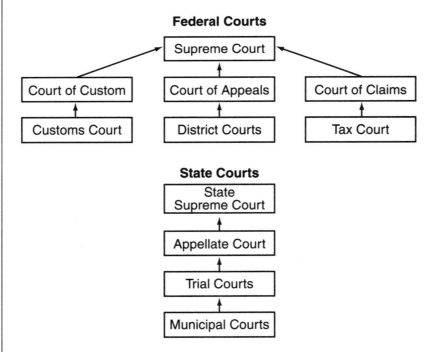

Federal Courts

Supreme Court

Court of Custom | Court of Appeals | Court of Claims
Customs Court | District Courts | Tax Court

State Courts

State Supreme Court

Appellate Court

Trial Courts

Municipal Courts

Lower courts may appeal a ruling to a higher court, as indicated by the direction of the arrows.

United States of America

A republic composed of fifty states and Washington, D.C. (the District of Columbia), the nation's capital. Forty-eight states are located in the continental U.S.A.; Alaska is west of Canada and Hawaii is in the South Pacific. The U.S.A. has coastlines on three oceans: the Atlantic, the Pacific, and the Arctic. In this land of contrasting environments, altitudes range from 282 feet below sea level in Death Valley, California, to 20,320 feet above sea level, the peak of Mt. McKinley in Alaska.

See also the list of the states on pages 178 and 179.

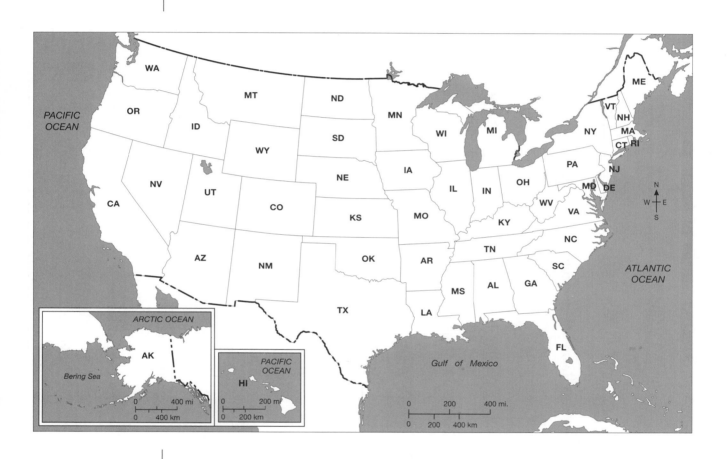

United States of America

State	Abbrev.	Capital	State Nickname	State Flower	State Bird	Admitted
Alabama	AL	Montgomery	Heart of Dixie	Camellia	Yellowhammer	1819
Alaska	AK	Juneau	Last Frontier	Forget-Me-Not	Willow Ptarmigan	1959
Arizona	AZ	Phoenix	Grand Canyon State	Saguaro	Cactus Wren	1912
Arkansas	AR	Little Rock	Land of Opportunity	Apple Blossom	Mockingbird	1836
California	CA	Sacramento	Golden State	Golden Poppy	California Valley Quail	1850
Colorado	CO	Denver	Centennial State	Rocky Mt. Columbine	Lark Bunting	1876
Connecticut*	CT	Hartford	Constitution State	Mountain Laurel	Robin	1788
Delaware*	DE	Dover	First State	Peach Blossom	Blue Hen Chicken	1787
Florida	FL	Tallahassee	Sunshine State	Orange Blossom	Mockingbird	1845
Georgia*	GA	Atlanta	Empire State of the South	Cherokee Rose	Brown Thrasher	1788
Hawaii	HI	Honolulu	Aloha State	Hibiscus	Hawaiian Goose	1959
Idaho	ID	Boise	Gem State	Syringa	Mountain Bluebird	1890
Illinois	IL	Springfield	Land of Lincoln	Native Violet	Cardinal	1818
Indiana	IN	Indianapolis	Hoosier State	Peony	Cardinal	1816
Iowa	IA	Des Moines	Hawkeye State	Wild Rose	Eastern Goldfinch	1846
Kansas	KS	Topeka	Sunflower State	Sunflower	Western Meadowlark	1861
Kentucky	KY	Frankfort	Bluegrass State	Goldenrod	Cardinal	1792
Louisiana	LA	Baton Rouge	Pelican State	Magnolia	Brown Pelican	1812
Maine	ME	Augusta	Pine Tree State	White Pine Cone	Chickadee	1820
Maryland*	MD	Annapolis	Old Line State	Black-eyed Susan	Baltimore Oriole	1788
Massachusetts*	MA	Boston	Bay State	Mayflower	Chickadee	1788
Michigan	MI	Lansing	Wolverine State	Apple Blossom	Robin	1837
Minnesota	MN	St. Paul	Gopher State	Lady's Slipper	Loon	1858
Mississippi	MS	Jackson	Magnolia State	Magnolia	Mockingbird	1817
Missour	MO	Jefferson City	Show Me State	Hawthorn	Bluebird	1821
Montana	MT	Helena	Treasure State	Bitterroot	Western Meadowlark	1889

United States of America (cont.)

State	Abbrev.	Capital	State Nickname	State Flower	State Bird	Admitted
Nebraska	NE	Lincoln	Cornhusker State	Goldenrod	Western Meadowlark	1867
Nevada	NV	Carson City	Silver State	Sagebrush	Mountain Bluebird	1864
New Hampshire*	NH	Concord	Granite State	Purple Lilac	Purple Finch	1788
New Jersey*	NJ	Trenton	Garden State	Purple Violet	Eastern Goldfinch	1787
New Mexico	NM	Santa Fe	Land of Enchantment	Yucca	Roadrunner	1912
New York*	NY	Albany	Empire State	Rose	Bluebird	1788
North Carolina*	NC	Raleigh	Tar Heel State	Dogwood	Cardinal	1789
North Dakota	ND	Bismarck	Flickertail State	Wild Prairie Rose	Western Meadowlark	1889
Ohio	OH	Columbus	Buckeye State	Scarlet Carnation	Cardinal	1803
Oklahoma	OK	Oklahoma City	Sooner State	Mistletoe	Scissortail Flycatcher	1907
Oregon	OR	Salem	Beaver State	Oregon Grape	Western Meadowlark	1859
Pennsylvania*	PA	Harrisburg	Keystone State	Mountain Laurel	Ruffed Grouse	1787
Rhode Island*	RI	Providence	Little Rhody	Violet	Rhode Island Red	1790
South Carolina*	SC	Columbia	Palmetto State	Carolina Jessamine	Carolina Wren	1788
South Dakota	SD	Pierre	Coyote State	American Pasqueflower	Ring-necked Pheasant	1889
Tennessee	TN	Nashville	Volunteer State	Iris	Mockingbird	1796
Texas	TX	Austin	Lone Star State	Bluebonnet	Mockingbird	1845
Utah	UT	Salt Lake City	Beehive State	Sego Lily	Sea Gull	1896
Vermont	VT	Montpelier	Green Mountain State	Red Clover	Hermit Thrush	1791
Virginia*	VA	Richmond	Old Dominion	Dogwood	Cardinal	1788
Washington	WA	Olympia	Evergreen State	Coast Rhododendron	Willow Goldfinch	1889
West Virginia	WV	Charleston	Mountain State	Rhododendron	Cardinal	1863
Wisconsin	WI	Madison	Badger State	Wood Violet	Robin	1848
Wyoming	WY	Cheyenne	Equality State	Indian Paintbrush	Meadowlark	1890

* Indicates one of the 13 original states

Venn diagram | An illustration using overlapping circles to show the relationship between sets, objects, or subjects in order to compare the similarities and differences of the items.

Example:

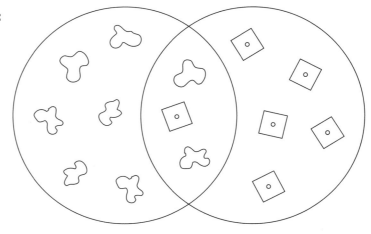

verb | A word that shows action or state-of-being (what the subject is).

Action	State of Being
sell	is
help	are
jump	am
eat	seem

Present Tense

▶ In the present tense, verbs tell about something that is happening or exists now.

▶ If the subject is first or second person singular, do not add an ending to the verb.

Examples: I *swim* in the pool today.
You *run* in the park in the morning.

▶ If the subject is third person singular, add *s* to the verb.

Examples: She *sings* today.
He *plays* baseball today.

Exception: Add *es* to verbs ending in *s, x, z, ch, sh*, or *ss*.

Examples: Cory *boxes* daily.
She *pushes* the stroller.

▶ If the subject is plural, do not add an *s* to the verb.

Examples: We *swim* in the lake.
Sally and Kevin *exercise* daily.

Helping Verbs

▶ Some verbs are helping verbs.

Some Common Helping Verbs

am	do	might
are	does	must
can	is	shall
could	may	should

Example: Jack *should eat* his dinner.

Past Tense

▶ Some verbs in the present tense help the *-ing* form of the main verb and show continuing action.

Example: Eddie *is painting* the walls.

▶ In the past tense, verbs show something that has already happened. The letters *d* or *ed* are added to regular verbs to form the past tense.

Examples: bake   bak*ed*
jump   jump*ed*

▶ If a verb ends with a consonant followed by *y*, change the *y* to *i* and add *ed*.

Examples: worry   worr*ied*
          hurry   hurr*ied*
          fry   fr*ied*

▶ If a verb ends in a vowel followed by a consonant, double the consonant and add *ed*.

Examples: stop   stop*ped*
          beg   beg*ged*
          prefer   prefer*red*
          omit   omit*ted*

Exceptions: enter   enter*ed*
             offer   offer*ed*

Helping Verbs

▶ Use the helping verbs *has*, *have*, or *had* with the past participle form of a verb to show that something *happened in the past*.

Examples: Sara *has played* ball before.
          Paul and Kathy *have seen* that movie.
          Karen *had showered* earlier.

verb, irregular

A verb that changes its spelling in the past tense and past participle form and does not have the *-ed* form.

Example:	**Present**	**Past**	**Past Participle**
	I drive.	Yesterday I drove.	I have driven.

Some Common Irregular Verbs

Present	Past	Past Participle
begin	began	begun
blow	blew	blown
bring	brought	brought
choose	chose	chosen
do	did	done
draw	drew	drawn
drink	drank	drunk
eat	ate	eaten
go	went	gone
grow	grew	grown
lay	laid	laid (to set)
lie	lay	lain (to rest)
ring	rang	rung
swim	swam	swum
wake	woke	woken

vertex The endpoint where two lines (rays) meet, forming an angle. When reading the letters of an angle, the middle letter names the vertex. The plural of vertex is *vertices.*

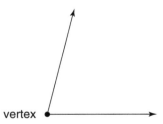

vertical line A line that runs straight up and down, perpendicular to the horizon.

Example:

volcano | An opening in the earth's crust through which lava, ash, dust, and hot gases are thrown out.

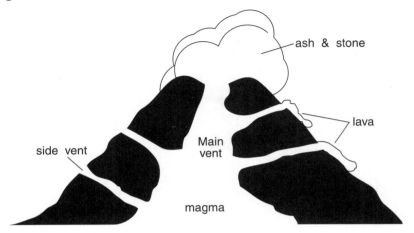

volume | The amount of space inside a solid figure, usually measured by cubic centimeters, cubic inches, cubic feet, or cubic yards.

▶ To find the volume of a cube or rectangular prism, multiply the length times the width times the height.

$V = L \times W \times H$
$V = 4" \times 2" \times 2"$
$V = 16$ cu. in.

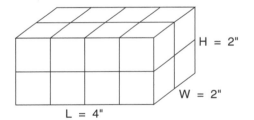

vowel | Any letter of the alphabet that is not a consonant and sometimes *w* and *y*.

Long Vowel Sounds		Short Vowel Sounds	
a	ape	a	cat
e	equal	e	hen
i	ice	i	pig
o	open	o	otter
u	use	u	cub
y	fly		

vowel digraph | *See* **digraph.**

weather/whether

The word *weather* refers to atmospheric conditions.

    Example: The *weather* will be cold and wet on Monday.

The word *whether* suggests a question.

    Example: I don't know *whether* she will go.

webbing

A visual method of organizing thoughts and ideas before putting them into story or report form. Each arm of the topic can be a new paragraph.

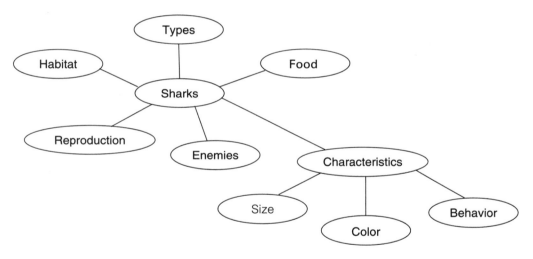

well

See **good/well.**

we're/where/were

The word *we're* is a contraction that means "we are."

    Example: *We're* in the kitchen.

The word *where* is an adverb that tells or asks location.

    Example: Do you know *where* the cat is?

The word *were* is a past tense form of the verb "to be."

> **Example:** We *were* in school yesterday.

who-whom

The word *who* is used as the subject of a sentence or a clause.

> **Example:** *Who* did that?   Can you tell *who* did it?

The word *whom* is the objective case (object of a verb or preposition) of *who*.

> **Example:** *Whom* did you *ask* to the dance?
> *To whom* will the package be sent?

whole number

An integer. Any number in the set (0, 1, 2, 3, ...)

See also **integer.**

world

The earth. The world is round. The circumference of the world at the equator is 24,902 miles (40,075 kilometers). The circumference when measured around the world at the poles is 24,860 miles (40,007 kilometers).

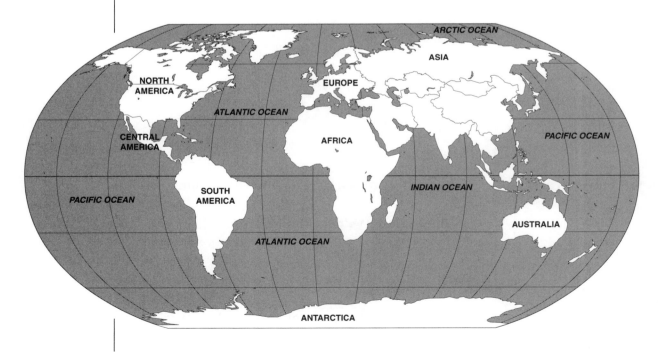

writer's word list | An alternative word list to commonly used words.

People

accomplice, alien, ancestor, angel, audience, bandit, beauty, braggart, bungler, cad, chap, clique, clod, coward, culprit, delinquent, dwarf, emigrant, enemy, expert, fake, fiend, foe, fraud, freak, genius, glutton, gnome, good-for-nothing, gossip, gourmet, grouch, hag, hero/heroine, idol, imp, imposter, intruder, infant, liar, miser, monster, native, newcomer, nymph, oaf, ogre, onlooker, outcast, outlaw, outsider, partner, pauper, pest, pushover, rascal, ragamuffin, rebel, rival, runt, scoundrel, show-off, shrew, snob, snoop, stick-in-the-mud, tattler, tourist, underdog, urchin, vagabond, veteran, waif, weakling, wizard

Places

abode, abroad, arena, atmosphere, attic, balcony, bazaar, belfry, bleachers, cafe, cellar, chamber, cliff, coast, corridor, den, depot, dungeon, frontier, gallery, gutter, hang-out, harbor, haven, hilltop, inn, lair, lagoon, lobby, lodge, loft, lounge, madhouse, mall, mansion, mill, niche, nook, outlet, parlor, passageway, port, post, retreat, ruin, temple, tower, tunnel, shelter, shrine, swamp, warehouse, wharf

Time

afternoon, afterwards, annually, beforehand, briefly, bygone, current, daily, dawn, daybreak, dragging, dusk, endless, era, eternity, evening, flash, formerly, frequently, future, gradually, hastily, hurried, immediate, indefinitely, instantly, intermission, interruption, lapse, lastly, let-up, lifetime, lull, meanwhile, moment, nightly, pause, period, permanent, present, rapidly, recent, shortly, swiftly, timely, up-to-date

Sight

ablaze, aged, beaming, bedraggled, blur, brilliant, complexion, crystal, dappled, dim, dingy, drab, dull, dusky, faded, fiery, flaming, flicker, flushed, fuzzy, gaudy, glare, glassy, gleam, glimmer, glisten, gloomy, grimy, grubby, hue, iridescent, lustre, mangy, milky, mottled, mousy, muddy, multicolored, murky, opaque, pasty, red-hot, rich, rosy, ruddy, sallow, sheen, shimmer, slinky, speckled, stain, swarthy, transparent, trim, twinkle, vibrant, vivid, watery

blink, browse, face, focus, gape, gawk, gaze, glance, glimpse, inspect, leaf, monitor, peek, peep, scan, scout, scrutinize, skim, snoop, squint, stare, view

Odor

aroma, bouquet, fragrant, incense, musty, odorless, peppery, perfumed, putrid, pungent, rancid, rank, reek, scent, sharp, sour, sniff, stale, whiff

Sound

bang, bark, buzz, cackle, chant, clatter, clink, crank, crunch, din, drone, echo, flutter, howl, gasp, grate, gurgle, hoarse, husky, jangle, mellow, muffled, peal, rumble, rustle, screech, shriek, shrill, sizzle, snicker, squawk, wail, whimper, whine, whoop, yowl

Speech

address, ad-lib, alarm, babble, beckon, bicker, bid, blab, blurt, boast, chat, chatter, comment, converse, gab, grumble, heckle, hush, improvise, jabber, jaw, lecture, mince, moan, mutter, pant, parrot, preach, quibble, ramble, rant, rap, recite, reply, recount, sermonize, slur, snap, spout, squabble, stammer, taunt, utter, vocalize, whisper, yap, yelp, yodel

Touch

brittle, bumpy, bushy, clammy, crisp, crumbly, crusty, damp, fiery, firm, flabby, fleecy, fluffy, frosty, gooey, gritty, gummy, hairy, icy, knobby, lukewarm, jagged, matted, mushy, parched, plush, powdery, rocky, silky, sleek, spongy, taut, threadbare

Taste

appetizing, bitter, blah, bland, consume, delectable, devour, flavorful, luscious, nibble, peck, peppery, piquant, pungent, rancid, savory, scrumptious, sour, spicy, stale, sugar-coated

writing process   The steps taken to develop and complete a written work.

Prewriting: Deciding on a topic to write about by listing all of the ideas that interest you.

Brainstorming: Once a topic has been decided upon, writing down all of the words that remind you of your topic, followed by making a web or an outline.

First draft: Rough writing of a story; a way to put ideas into sentences and paragraphs without being concerned about incorrect spelling or punctuation. Ideas can be added or deleted.

Revision: Changing the parts of the writing that do not keep to the important points of the report or story. Does the work include a beginning, middle, and ending? Self-evaluation and peer-conferencing are done at this point.

Editing/proofreading: Checking for spelling, grammar, and punctuation errors; checking for continuity and organization of information and ideas.

Final draft: Completing the work by typing it or handwriting it in your neatest writing. A final check for all errors is done. This is a good time for illustrations to be included.

Publishing: Publishing your work to allow other people to read your report or story for knowledge and enjoyment.

Z

zip code

A system designed to simplify and speed the delivery of mail by assigning a five-digit number to each delivery area in the United States.

zodiac

An imaginary band in the sky showing the paths of the sun, moon, and planets and divided into twelve areas. The twelve divisions have the names of the constellations: Capricorn, Aquarius, Pisces, Aries, Taurus, Gemini, Cancer, Leo, Virgo, Libra, Scorpio, and Sagittarius.

Activity Pages

Robot for Sale

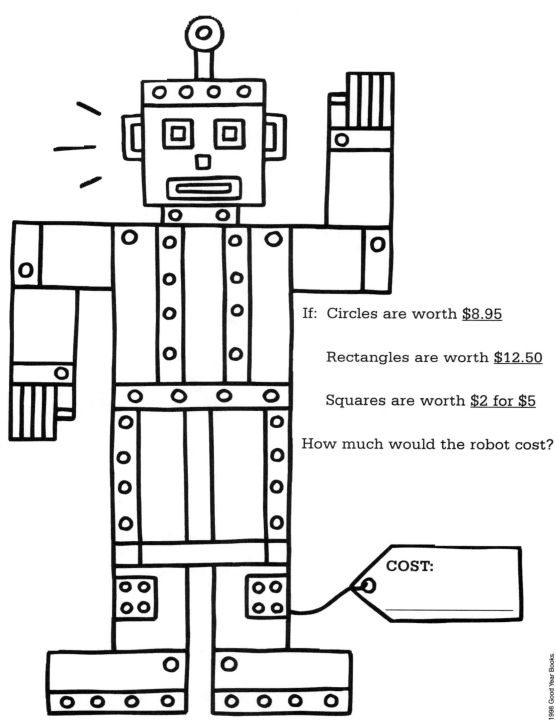

If: Circles are worth $8.95

Rectangles are worth $12.50

Squares are worth $2 for $5

How much would the robot cost?

COST: _____

Space Mix-Up

There's trouble in outer space! The planets are out of their orbits and can't seem to get back where they belong. Draw each planet in its right place. Tell how many millions of miles each planet is from the sun.

Write below the easy way to remember the order of the planets starting with the sun.

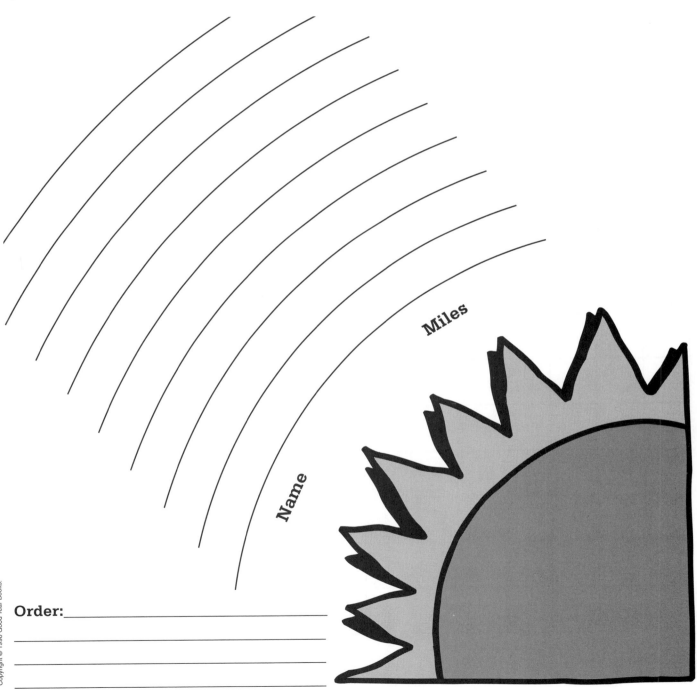

Miles

Name

Order:_____

_____

_____

_____

Presidential Name Game

Use this grid to create a pattern using any president's last name.
Write the name of your choice across the top line of the grid.
Leave the next square following the name blank. If the president's
name is 6 letters, you will need 7 squares across and 7 squares
going down. Cut away the rest of the grid. Begin writing the name
again in the first blank square and continue to repeat writing the
name until you have finished filling in the grid.

Color all the same letters one color to create a name pattern. See the
example at the right for an illustration of a finished grid.

P	O	L	K	P
O	L	K	P	O

When would the pattern begin to repeat itself?

_____

_____

_____

_____

Why?

_____

_____

_____

_____

You are the copyeditor of *The Alien Post,* a daily newspaper on the planet Zeni. You need to proofread the following story before it can go to press. Use a colored pencil and proofreading symbols to make the corrections. Write a headline for the story.

Deliveries Anywhere in Outer Space

Have you ever wondered if there was life on Earth During a regular exploratory space mision Zeninauts spotted odd-looking creetures assumed to be Earthlings. unlike zenites these strange beings ap peared too have only one headsphere two sight orbs and an unusual speaker cavity which seemed at tached to there hearing sensors by a device into which they spoke. Even more strange were the tiny thread-like strands riseing out of the

tops of thier headspheres Sometimes these threads were adorned with shi ny ribbons or small bars. but the strangist sight of all were the large white laced coverings much of the Population wore on there transporter pads The next space venture is scheduled next next year. The Zeninauts are eager to make return mission to see what else they can learn about Earthlings

What custom do Earthlings have that you think Zenites might find unusual or interesting? Draw a picture on the other side of your paper.

Calendar Caper

The year 1996 was a leap year. In the first calendar below, complete the next leap year calendar page for February 1996 by filling in the year, days, and dates. In the second calendar, complete the calendar page for February of the next leap year. Be careful—it looks easier than it is!

Tessie the Tessellator

Tessie enjoys creating different tessellations. Help her design four new patterns. Use squares, rectangles, or triangles to create the designs, and then have fun coloring them.

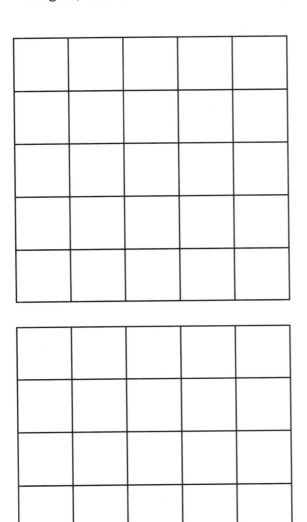

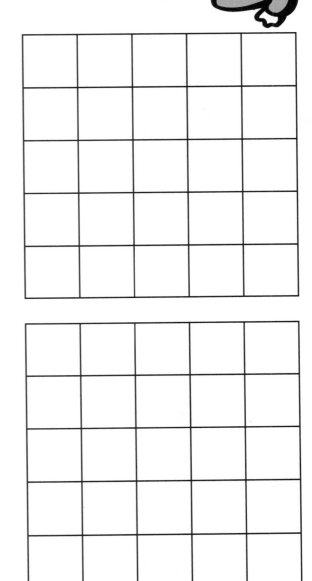

Name six places where your new tesselations might be used.

_____   _____

_____   _____

_____   _____

Foreign Phrases

These common foreign phrases are often found in the books we read. Use the picture clues to help you match the correct phrase to the picture.

1 and 2 and 3, etc.		
_____	_____	_____
Samuel Clemens	A B C D J K L M E F G H	1995, 1996, 1997, 1998, 1999, 2000
_____	_____	_____
BURP!		SALE BARGAIN
_____	_____	_____

Geo Quiz

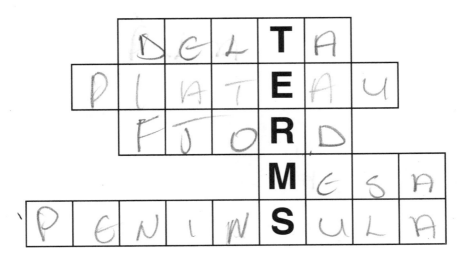

Use the words in the list below to complete the puzzle grid.

plateau
mountain
delta
channel
archipelago
gulf
mesa
horizon
peninsula
desert
oasis
isthmus
fjord
glacier
canyon

G U L F
D **E** S E R T
C A N Y **O** N
G L A C I E R
H O **R** I Z O N
M O U N T **A** I N
A R C H I **P** E L A G O
I S T **H** M U S
O A S **I** S
C H A N N E L

D E L **T** A
P L A T **E** A U
F J O **R** D
M E S A
P E N I N **S** U L A

Tim's Time

Complete the time line with Tim's daily routine.
Add two more activities to Tim's busy schedule.

Tim's Day

lunch	after-school snack
take bus home	eat breakfast
eat dinner	morning recess
get up	bedtime
afternoon art	morning math
brush teeth	get dressed
alarm rings	do homework

1. take bus to school   2. English

8:00 A.M.   **8:00 P.M.**

lunch

Put Tim's daily routine in alphabetical order, including the two activities you added.

ALARM RING	Morning MATH	after school snack
GET UP	Morning Recess	do homework
EAT Breakfast	English	EAT dinner
BRUSH TEETH	Lunch	Bed TIMe
GET DRESSED	Afternoon Art	
TAke bus to school	Take bus Home	

Mixed-Up Milly

Mixed-up Milly always muddled everything she did. Milly's mother made a marvelous milkshake and told Milly to share it with her friends, Mimi, Matty, and Marcy. Milly wanted to be sure she gave her friends an equal amount. Each girl held an empty quart container except for Milly; hers was full. Her friends decided to help her. Did each girl get an equal amount, or did Milly muddle again?

- Milly poured 1/2 of her container into Mimi's.
- Mimi gave 1/2 of her milkshake to Matty.
- Milly gave 1/2 of hers to Matty.
- Mimi poured 1/2 of her milkshake into Matty's container.
- Marcy asked for 1/2 of Mimi's milkshake.
- Milly poured all of her milkshake into Marcy's container.
- Matty gave all of her milkshake to Milly.
- One cup of Marcy's container was given to Milly.
- Milly poured one cup of her milkshake into Mimi's container.
- Mimi gave 1/4 cup to Marcy.
- Milly poured 1 1/2 cups of hers into Matty's container.
- Matty poured 1/2 cup into Marcy's container.

How much did each girl get?

Milly _____ Mimi _____ Matty _____ Marcy _____

Did Mixed-up Milly muddle? _____

Polygon Pete

Help Peter draw a polygon that has 4 sides, 2 squares, and 8 triangles.
Sound easy? Here's the catch. You may draw only 8 lines!

Picture This

Create a work of art using geometric figures. The side of one figure must touch the side of the figure next to it. See how many different figures you can use.

State the State

Read the clues given for each state. Match the clues with the name of the correct state. Write the name of the state and the clue letter under the state outline.

Name: _____ _____

Clue: _____ _____

Name: _____ _____

Clue: _____ _____

Name: _____ _____

Clue: _____ _____

Name: _____ _____

Clue: _____ _____

a. Ponce De Leon named this state "flowery"; second longest coastline; state flower: orange blossom.

b. More than 15,000 lakes; named from a Sioux word meaning "cloudy water"; Gopher State.

c. Only state named for a president; capital: Olympia; Grand Coulee Dam.

d. Named from the Sioux word *Quapaw* meaning "downstream people"; state bird: mockingbird.

e. Silver State; mostly mountains and desert; state flower: sagebrush.

f. The first capital of the U.S.; originally named New Netherland.

g. Called Magnolia State; named from Chippewa word meaning "father of the waters"; admitted to the union 1817.

h. Largest working gold mine in U.S.; Mt. Rushmore; called Coyote State.

When, Where, How?

Help the clown color the adverb balloons.
Use red for the adverb balloons that tell WHEN.
Use yellow for the adverb balloons that tell WHERE.
Use green for the adverb balloons that tell HOW.
Use any other color for the adverb balloons that tell TO WHAT EXTENT, and draw a wavy line through them.

Mama Mia, It's Onomatopoeia

Unscramble the words. Then draw a picture that describes the word.

zubz

Buzz

opw

Pow

hwew

Whew

hracs

CRASH

whiss

paz

ZAP

ltieshr

gnab

BANG

Short Stuff

Can you find the words that these abbreviations represent? The words can be found going up, down, backward, and diagonally. Use a colored pencil or light colored marker.

lb.	Mrs.	doz.	qt.
Blvd.	oz.	A.D.	n.
in.	Ave.	gal.	Rd.
m.p.h.	P.S.	ht.	pt.
anon.	etc.	v.	A.M.

E	T	C	E	T	E	R	A	R	D	L	T	A	B
M	I	L	E	S	P	E	R	H	O	U	R	A	F
I	T	N	I	P	B	Q	E	B	Z	M	A	G	E
S	H	A	Z	R	O	G	O	P	E	H	U	A	U
T	G	R	E	C	N	U	O	T	N	C	Q	L	N
R	I	V	M	H	L	A	N	O	U	N	U	L	E
E	E	X	F	E	R	O	A	D	Q	I	T	O	V
S	H	C	V	D	S	U	O	M	Y	N	O	N	A
S	L	A	N	T	E	M	E	R	I	D	I	E	M
W	R	E	L	I	N	I	M	O	D	O	N	N	A
D	O	Z	R	T	P	I	R	C	S	T	S	O	P

Answer Key

Robot for Sale

52 circles	$465.40	–	$465.40
48 – 55 rectangles	600.00	–	688.00
12 – 16 squares	30.00	–	40.00
	$1,095.40	–	$1,193.40

Space Mix-Up

Following is a list of the planets and their distance, in miles from the sun.

Mercury	36,000,000
Venus	67,000,000
Earth	93,000,000
Mars	141,000,000
Jupiter	483,000,000
Saturn	888,000,000
Uranus	1,785,000,000
Neptune	2,795,000,000
Pluto	3,666,000,000

My **V**ery **E**asy **M**ethod—**J**ust **S**et **U**p **N**ine **P**lanets

Alien Post

Column 1
Line 1 paragraph symbol
Line 2 Earth.
Line 4 (sp) mission
Line 6 (sp) creatures
Line 7 (cap) Unlike
Line 8 (cap) Zenite,
Line 9 (space) appeared; (sp) to
Line 10 headspheres
Line 11 orbs,
Line 13 (space) attached; (sp) their

Column 2
Line 3 (sp) rising
Column 3
Line 1 (sp) their; headspheres.
Line 3 (space) shiny
Line 4 (cap) But
Line 5 (sp) strangest
Line 6 large, white
Line 8 (lower case) population; (sp) their
Line 9 pads.
Line 11 delete one *next*
Line 13 insert *a*
Line 15 Earthlings.

Calendar Caper

The next leap year is 2000, and Leap Day, February 29, 2000, will be a Tuesday.

Foreign Phrases

per capita, nom de plume, faux pas, tempus fugit, non sequiter, déjà vu, ex libre, per annum, caveat emptor

Geo Quiz

```
          G U L F
          D E S E R T
    C A N Y O N
            G L A C I E R
        H O R I Z O N
  M O U N T A I N
  A R C H I P E L A G O
      I S T H M U S
      O A S I S
          C H A N N E L

      D E L T A
    P L A T E A U
      F J O R D
          M E S A
  P E N I N S U L A
```

Mixed-Up Millie

Each girl has 1 cup.
No.

Polygon Pete

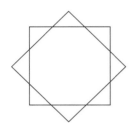

State the State

Minnesota
b.

Nevada
e.

New York
f.

Washington
c.

Arkansas
d.

South Dakota
h.

Florida
a.

Mississippi
g.

When, Where, How

When (red): often/frequently/recently/
early/immediately
Where (yellow): inside/nowhere/upward/
nearby/outside/there/here
How (green): carefully/quietly/rudely/
quickly/slowly/easily
To What Extent (any color):
very/most/almost/never more/extremely

Mama Mia

buzz; pow; whew; crash; swish; zap;
slither; bang

Short Stuff

E	T	C	E	T	E	R	A	R	D	L	T	A	B
M	I	L	E	S	P	E	R	H	O	U	R	A	F
I	T	N	I	P	B	Q	E	B	Z	M	A	G	E
S	H	A	Z	R	O	G	O	P	E	H	U	A	U
T	G	R	E	C	N	U	O	T	N	C	Q	L	N
R	I	V	M	H	L	A	N	O	U	N	U	L	E
E	E	X	F	E	R	O	A	D	Q	I	T	O	V
S	H	C	V	D	S	U	O	M	Y	N	O	N	A
S	L	A	N	T	E	M	E	R	I	D	I	E	M
W	R	E	L	I	N	I	M	O	D	O	N	N	A
D	O	Z	R	T	P	I	R	C	S	T	S	O	P

Index

Astronomy

Constellation, 53

Galaxy, 77

Milky Way, 111

Planet, 131

Solar System, 156

Zodiac, 189

Computer

Computer Words, 49

Internet Words, 94

Earth Science

Atmospheric Layers, 19

Bedrock, 23

Continents, 53

  Map, 54

Core, 55

Crust, 56

Ecology, 68

Fault, 72

Geographic Terms, 78

Geography, 80

Glacier, 82

Great Lakes, 83

Hemisphere, 88

Hydrosphere, 89

Igneous Rock, 91

Lava, 98

Magma, 105

Mantle, 106

Mass, 107

Meridian, 110

Metamorphic Rock, 110

Mineral, 111

Ocean, 121

Ozone Layer, 123

Pangaea, 123

Sedimentary Rock, 154

Tectonic Plates. 170

Tides, 172

Tropic of Cancer, 175

Tropic of Capricorn, 175

Volcano, 184

Government

Bill of Rights, 24

Cabinet, 28

District of Columbia, 64

Presidential Succession Order, 138

Presidents of the United States, 139

United States Court System, 176

Grammar

Abbreviation, 2

Adjective, 5

Adverb, 6

Antecedent, 12

Article, 18

Can/May, 31

Clause, 41

Compound Sentence, 48

Compound Subject, 48

Conjunction, 52

Contraction, 55

Declarative Sentence, 59

Exclamatory Sentence, 70

Good/Well, 82

I/Me, 90

Imperative Sentence, 91

Interjection, 93

Interrogative Sentence, 95

Irregular Verb, 96

Italics, 96

Its/It's, 96

Lay/Lie, 99

Learn/Teach, 99

Let/Leave, 100

Noun, 118

Parenthetical Expression, 125

Parts of Speech, 126

Past Tense, 126

Plural, 133

Possessive Nouns, 135

Predicate, 135

Present Tense, 137

Quotation, 146

Quotation Marks, 146

Singular, 156

Subject, 164

Subject/Verb Agreement, 164

Than/Then, 171

Their/There/They're, 171

To/Too/Two, 175

Weather/Whether, 185

We're/Where/Were, 185

Who/Whom, 186

History

Colonies, 44

Greek Gods and Goddesses, 84

Northwest Territory, 117

Presidents of the United States, 139

States, 162

Library Skills

Book Parts, 25

Dewey Decimal System, 60

Library of Congress
Classification System, 103

Literature

Cliché, 42

Foreign Words and Phrases, 74

Parable, 124

Prose, 144

Proverb, 145

Satire, 152

Sonnet, 158

Map Study

Atlas, 19

Compass Rose, 47

Key, 97

Latitude, 98

Legend, 100

Longitude, 105

Map, 106

Map Scale of Miles, 107

Meridian, 110

Prime Meridian, 140

States, 162

United States of America, 177

World, 186

Mathematics

Addition

Addend, 4

Addition, 4

Associative Property, 18

Average, 20

Carrying, 36

Casting Out Nines, 37

Commutative Property, 47

Fact Family, 71

Magic Square, 105

Mean, 108

Sum, 166

Decimal

Decimal, 56

Fraction/Decimal Equivalents, 57

Fraction to Decimal, 76

Percent, 126

Division

Average, 20

Casting Out Nines, 37

Denominator, 60

Dividend, 64

Divisibility, 64

Division, 66

Divisor, 67

Least Common Denominator, 99

Mean, 108

Numerator, 120

Quotient, 147

Ratio, 148

Remainder, 149

Square Root, 162

Fraction

Fraction, 75

Fraction/Decimal Equivalents, 57

Fraction to Decimal, 76

Fraction Number Line, 76

Improper Fraction, 91

Mixed Number, 111

Rational Number, 148

General Math

Algorithm, 7

Attribute, 19

Average, 20

Brackets, 28

Calculator, 29

Concave, 51

Convex, 55

Estimate, 70

Flow Chart, 73

Greater Than, 83

Less Than, 100

Math Symbols, 108

Mean, 108

Number Sentence, 119

Probability, 141

Properties of Numbers, 144

Reciprocal, 148

Roman Numerals, 150

Rounding, 151

Tangram, 170

Tessellation, 171

Geometry

Angle

Acute, 3

Adjacent, 5

Angle, 10

Horizontal Line, 88

Hypotenuse, 90

Intersecting Lines, 96

Line Segment, 104

Perpendicular Lines, 130

Protractor, 144

Quadrant, 145

Quadrilateral, 145

Parallelogram, 80

Rectangle, 81

Rhombus, 81

Square, 81

Trapezoid, 81

Ray, 148
  Straight, 163
  Supplementary, 167
  Triangle, 81
  Equilateral, 80
  Isosceles, 80
  Right, 150
  Scalene, 81
  Vertex, 183
  Vertical Line, 183
Apex, 12
Asymmetric, 18
Circle, 40
  Arc, 16
  Circumference, 40
  Chord, 40
  Diameter, 61
  Pi, 130
  Radius, 148
  Sector, 153
Closed Figure, 43
Concentric Circles, 51
Cone, 80
Cube, 80
Cylinder, 80
Geometric Figures, 80
Hexagon, 80
N-gon, 117
Oblong, 120
Octagon, 80
Parallel Lines, 125
Pentagon, 81
Prism
  Rectangular, 81
  Triangular, 81
Rectangle, 81
Graphs/Grids
  Axis, 20

Bar Graph, 82
Circle Graph, 82
Coordinates, 55
Diagram, 60
Graph, 82
Grid, 85
Line Graph, 82
Number Pair, 119
Ordered Pair, 121
Symmetry, 169
Venn Diagram, 180
Measurement
  Area, 17
  Array, 17
  Capacity, 31
  Centimeter, 39
  Degree, 59
  Measurement Chart, 109
  English/Metric Conversion
Table, 68
  Metric/English Conversion
Table, 111
  Perimeter, 128
  Volume, 184
Money
  Annuity, 12
  Bank Check, 21
  Capital, 31
  Compound Interest, 48
  Dividend, 64
  Gross, 85
  Interest, 93
  Money, 112
  Net Profit, 117
  Simple Interest, 156
  Stock Market, 162
Multiplication
  Associative Property, 18

Casting Out Nines, 37
Common Factor, 47
Commutative Property, 47
Distributive Property, 64
Exponent, 70
Factor Tree, 71
Greatest Common Factor, 83
Lattice Multiplication, 98
Minuend, 111
Multiple, 116
Multiplicand, 113
Multiplication Table, 114
Multiplier, 116
Product, 141
Place Value
  Cardinal Number, 35
  Digit, 63
  Even Number, 70
  Expanded Numeral, 70
  Googol, 82
  Integer, 93
  Negative Number, 117
  Number Line, 119
  Number Prefixes, 119
  Numeral, 119
  Odd Number, 121
  Ordinal Number, 122
  Place Value, 131
  Prime Number, 140
  Unit, 176
  Whole Number, 186
Subtraction
  Borrowing, 27
  Casting Out Nines, 37
  Difference, 62
  Fact Family, 71
  Minuend, 111
  Subtrahend, 165

Music

Clef, 42

Musical Expressions, 116

Musical Note and Rest Values, 116

Note/Piano Keyboard Relationship, 118

Octave, 121

Pitch, 131

Scale, 152

Staff, 162

Poetry

Ballad, 21

Cinquain, 40

Diamonte, 61

Haiku, 87

Limerick, 104

Quatrain, 145

Punctuation

Apostrophe, 13

Capital Letter, 31

Colon, 44

Comma, 44

Hyphen, 89

Initial, 92

Parentheses, 125

Period, 128

Preposition, 137

Prepositional Phrase, 137

Pronoun, 142

Semicolon, 154

Verb, 180

Verb, Irregular, 180

Reading

Accent Mark, 3

Analogy, 10

Antonym, 13

Appendix, 16

Appositive, 16

Base Word, 22

Blend, 25

Book Report, 26

Compound Word, 49

Consonant, 52

Consonant Cluster, 53

Digraph, 63

Fact or Opinion, 71

Fiction, 72

Glossary, 82

Guide Words, 86

Homograph, 88

Homonym, 88

Homophone, 88

Hyperbole, 89

Idiom, 91

Inference, 92

Key Words, 97

Main Topic and Subtopics, 105

Metaphor, 110

Nonfiction, 117

Onomatopoeia, 121

Oxymoron, 123

Palindrome, 123

Personification, 130

Phrase, 130

Prefix, 136

Pronunciation Key, 142

Root Word, 151

Schwa, 152

Sequence, 155

Silent Letter, 155

Simile, 156

Spoonerism, 162

Stress Mark, 163

Story Elements, 163

Suffix, 166

Syllable, 167

Synonym, 169

Table of Contents, 170

Vowel, 184

Resource Books

Almanac, 8

Atlas, 19

Dictionary, 62

Encyclopedia, 68

Thesaurus, 172

Science

Animal Offspring, 12

Axis, 20

Celsius Thermometer, 39

Clouds, 43

Digestive System, 62

Fahrenheit Thermometer, 72

Food Pyramid, 73

Fossil, 75

Oxidation, 123

Periodic Table of Elements, 129

Photosynthesis, 130

Richter Scale, 150

Solstice, 156

Thermometer, 172

Spelling

A/An/And, 1

Accept/Except, 3

Affect/Effect, 7

All ready/Already, 7

All Together/Altogether, 7

Desert/Dessert, 60

Farther/Further, 72

Frequently Misspelled Word List, 161

Spelling Rules, 158

Time

A.D., 3

A.M., 9

B.C., 22

B.C.E., 23

B.P., 28

Calendar, 29

Counterclockwise, 55

Days of the Week, 56

Greenwich Mean Time, 85

International Date Line, 94

Leap Year, 99

Light Year, 104

Months of the Year, 112

P.M., 135

Seasons of the Year, 153

Time, 172

Time Line, 172

Time Zones, 174

Writing Skills

Addressing an Envelope, 5

Alphabet, 8

Alphabetizing, 9

Autobiography, 19

Biography, 24

Business Letter, 101

Clustering, 44

Essay, 70

Footnote, 73

Friendly Letter, 102

Ibid., 90

Index, 92

Letter Writing, 101

Outline Form, 122

Paragraph, 124

Plot, 133

Proofreading, 143

Research Paper, 149

Run-on Sentence, 152

Sentence, 154

Subtopic, 164

Syntax, 169

Topic Sentence, 175

Underlining, 176

Webbing, 185

Writer's Word List, 187

Writing Process, 188